from Leigh-Brown

D0949308

This book is dedicated with much love

to my wonderful grandchildren

who are such fun—

Sabelo Samora, Harley Jonah, Aisha Grace,

Caitlin Faith, Siyanda Sandino,

Sesethu Romero

May they all enjoy God's revolution of love

CONTENTS

PREFACE

Somewhere around 4 B.C. the Prince of Peace was born. A word, a statement, an action, a lifestyle, a revolution of love burst with hope from Bethlehem—at the time, an occupied territory—showing us how to live as a kingdom or community of love.

Now Bethlehem is occupied territory once again. But a movement is being born again there from the followers of the Prince of Peace that says there is a better way, a nonviolent way. This community is sending a message of love and justice and peace, a prophecy that offers hope to the whole world.

■ ■ ■

I was appointed as a canon of St. George's Anglican Cathedral in Jerusalem by Bishop Riah Abu El-Assal, the previous bishop of Jerusalem. (He was succeeded by Bishop Suheil Dawani.) I thanked Bishop Riah very much for the appointment, and then I asked, "What does a canon do?"

"We would normally say, 'Tell our story,'" he responded, "but you have been telling our story in songs and in words. So continue to do that." I have learned from this church, whose members in Israel and Palestine are predominantly Palestinian, and so I feel the responsibility and the challenge to tell its story, to let their voices be heard. (I do this primarily in chapters two and four.)

When one talks about Palestine and Israel it is very easy to be accused of being on one side or the other. My commitment is for a win-win situation there. Our commitment at Amos Trust, and my commitment, is to be pro-Palestinian and pro-Israeli; we do not see it as a victory if one side dominates another. So we work toward the day when justice for the Palestinians will mean peace and security for both communities. I try to make sure that our views reflect those of our friends and partners, and particularly of the Christians who have put together the new Kairos Palestine document, which I will talk about in chapter four. But also I am reflecting the advice of Jewish and Muslim friends who have shown courage in their stand for justice.

The Amos Trust has become a significant human rights organization committed to justice and working with partners in Nicaragua, South Africa, India and Palestine/Israel. (I tell the story of the Amos Trust in appendix one.) Their stories appear throughout the book. We have learned from these partners how to live the gospel; they have helped us understand what the kingdom/community of God looks like in practice—they have made justice visible.

When Jeff Crosby of InterVarsity Press asked me to think about writing a book on justice, I was immediately interested, as Chris Rose, director of the Amos Trust, had just made a similar suggestion. I think it all comes together in this book. So thanks to Jeff and Chris. Thanks also to Dave Zimmerman, my editor, for all his helpful comments, and to Isobel, my assistant, for her typing, reading and helpful advice. Thanks to all the Amos team, staff and trustees. My thanks also to Rev. Dr. Jasmine Devadason for her piece on the prophet Amos that she wrote especially for the book. And also to those in Bethlehem and Jerusalem whom I interviewed for the book: Canon Naim Ateek, Sami Awad, Rev. Dr. Mitri Raheb, Zoughbi Zoughbi and Dr. Mazin Qumsiyeh.

Writing books can be quite unsociable, so much love and special thanks as always to my wife, Gill, for support, much tolerance and many good ideas.

■ ■ ■

Bethlehem is surrounded by a wall that reaches twenty-five feet high. And yet once behind the wall you find that God is already present there—already present everywhere there are the oppressed or forgotten. God is present, often in secret, among Dalits in India, among street children and the rural poor, among refugees running from conflict, among asylum seekers, among victims of various kinds of discrimination and marginalization, among women and girls seeking basic human rights, among those struggling to make a living in economies dominated by the one percent—and the list could go on. The conspiracy of love born in Bethlehem makes itself known in these places and among these communities, and so when we go to meet them and stand with them, we find that God is already there, waiting for us to join them.

GOD LOVES JUSTICE

Justice is God's calling card that introduces the Kingdom of God.

JOEL EDWARDS,
International Director
for Micah Challenge

JUSTICE LIKE A RIVER

Justice like a river
Let it flow—let it flow
Good news for the poor
Let it flow—let it flow
Like a never failing stream
Of justice and of peace
Justice like a river
Let it flow—let it flow

Let's unite under one tree
Under the branches of the olive tree
Let's unite under one tree
Under the shadow of a tree of life

Mercy flowing strongly
Let it flow—let it flow
Healing love and peace
Let it flow—let it flow

Strength for the struggles
Dignity for all
Justice like a river
Let it flow—let it flow

Justice like a river
Let it flow—let it flow

One Sunday afternoon when I was sixteen, I went to hear
Martin Luther King Jr. speak in St. Paul's Cathedral, London, on
his way to Oslo to pick up the Nobel Peace Prize. It had a huge
impact on me and helped me to better understand the justice of
the gospel and the importance of affirming all people equally.
Civil rights and human rights are crucial bases for our society,
and we find them rooted in the Bible.

I remember what a profound effect this had on me because
of King's very complete presentation of the gospel. His sermon
was on the subject of right relationships, and his text was Reve-
lation 21:16: "the length and the breadth and the height of it
are equal" (KJV), words from John's vision that refer to the new
Jerusalem. King said that the new city God was building would
not be an unbalanced entity with caring virtues on one side
and degrading vices on the other. The most noble thing about
it would be its completeness, whereas the troubles of our
world are due to incompleteness. He said the *length* of someone's life is his or her self-understanding and the discovery of
self-fulfillment.

The second dimension, he said, is the *breadth*, which is the
concern for and identification with one's fellow human, the rec-
ognition of the oneness of humanity and the need for active
brotherly concern for the welfare of others.

The third dimension is *height*. King said that humans must

actively seek God. We were made for God, and we will be restless until we find rest in God.

He ended up by saying, "Love yourself, if that means healthy self-interest, this is the length of life. Love your neighbor as we are commanded to do; this is the breadth of life. And the greatest commandment: 'Love the Lord your God with all your heart, with all your soul and with all your mind and with all your strength,' this is the height of life."[1]

It seemed to me then, and it still seems to me now, to be a very complete presentation. Ever since then it has affected my thinking, my reading of the Bible, my understanding of the gospel's commitment to justice and, hopefully, the way I live. I am only yards from where I heard and saw Martin Luther King Jr. as I write this book, in my studio right by St. Paul's Cathedral. This book is an attempt to reflect how I have tried to live out what I heard that day and particularly the justice that was at its heart.

Two Ways to See God

I think there are two ways to look at God. One is something I have reflected in a morning prayer that has turned into a song called "God with Sleeves Rolled Up." Later we will see the other way—as God who stands with us.

GOD WITH SLEEVES ROLLED UP

God with sleeves rolled up
God in the noise and the rush
God most clearly in the pause
Give us the strength for today
And the courage for what must be done

You are God of the darkness
God of the evening star
You are also God of the light
God of the morning star
Thank you for this day

Hope, they say, is to hear
The music of the future
But faith, they say, is to dance
To dance to it today
So thank you for this day

Thank you for this day
A day to breathe and restore
A day to stop and think again
A brand new day of hope
Thank you for this day

God with sleeves rolled up
God in the noise and the rush
God most clearly in the pause
Give us the strength for today
And the courage for what must be done

"God with Sleeves Rolled Up" conveys the idea of a God of action, the God who has made the first step toward humanity. The God whose example gives hope, restores and gives us courage is very much the God reflected in the Nicaraguan Campesino Mass of Carlos Mejia Godoy, a passionate poet and performer. I have had the privilege of hearing him sing a couple of times when I have been in Nicaragua.

You are the God of the poor
The human and simple God

The God who sweats in the street
The God with the weathered face
That's why I can talk to you
The language my own people talk, .
Because God, you are the laborer God,
The worker Christ.

Hand in hand you walk with my people
you struggle in the fields and the city.

And from the Sanctus:

You are three times holy
you are three times just
Free us from the yoke
And give us liberty.[2]

This Nicaraguan Mass reflects a God who understands struggles, the God of justice. But it doesn't lose the poetic and creative understanding of God. As the creed recited during the mass says,

I firmly believe, Lord
that from your fertile thought
this whole world was born;
that from your artist's hand,
like a primativist painter,
all beauty flourished:
the stars and the moon
the little houses, lagoons
the little boats floating
down the river to the sea,
the immense coffee plantations,
the white cotton fields
and the forests mutilated

by the criminal axe. . . .
In you I trust,
Maker of thought and music,
Maker of the wind,
Maker of peace and love.

And this reminds me of that other aspect of God—the God who
stands with us.

THE GOD WHO DANCES

Henri Matisse is rumored to have said
That he'd only believe in a God
Who understood how to dance.
I believe you are the God of dance.

You are the God who moves in creation
You are interwoven throughout evolution
You are the God who dances at dawn
You are the sparkle of light
You are the rhythm of life
Moving in mysterious ways

I feel you dancing on the earth
I sense your whisper in the trees
I breathe your spirit on the wind
You are the rhythm of life
Moving in mysterious ways
But always dancing
You are the God who dances.

The "God with sleeves rolled up" challenges us to do the
same—to be the hands and feet of Jesus and make the com-

munity of God visible. But God is also the God who is always beside us, the God who suffers with us, the God who restores our hope. This is the God who gives us courage to be prophetic when we don't want to be.

This is also "the God who dances," the God who is interwoven throughout evolution, the God who dances at dawn and gives us hope for the new day. This is the God who inspires our creativity, our passion for justice and our joy as the values of the kingdom/community become visible and as the poor and oppressed are treated with dignity.

JUSTICE INSTEAD OF RIGHTEOUSNESS

In 1985 I founded the Amos Trust, a small, creative Christian human rights agency that works with vibrant grassroots partners around the world. One of those, Gustavo Parajon (1935–2011), was a great friend and inspiration to me and a key mentor to us in Amos Trust. A doctor, pastor and peacemaker in Nicaragua, Gustavo said,

> The Christian faith impels us to seek justice. We see this especially in Jesus' ministry, and in the message of the prophets, and so it is very clear that God loves justice. It is an integral part of the gospel. This is what Jesus did— ministering to the people that were marginalized and oppressed—ministering to the people that didn't count in his time.[3]

We need a living theology like this that changes us—a justice theology rooted in the way and teachings of Jesus and in the Hebrew prophets. Justice is mentioned more times in the Bible than we often realize—it just gets clouded by the way it is translated. Canon Naim Ateek (Palestinian Israeli theologian from East Jerusalem and director of the Sabeel Theology Group) has pointed out how the word *righteousness* in the Bible would be better translated *justice* in many instances both in the Hebrew Scriptures and the New Testament. We usually understand the word *righteousness* as having an individual, personal aspect, whereas the meaning is social and political, not only personal. It identifies how we should live and care for one another in society.

This is highly significant, perhaps the key point for helping us understand the way of Jesus and the kingdom of God. So when we then think about the words from the Sermon on the Mount, "Blessed are those who hunger and thirst for *justice*, for they will be filled," the use of *justice* adds a different understanding and challenge—it sets those words alight.

Matthew 5:10 is equally powerful: "Blessed are those who are persecuted for *justice* sake." And then in Matthew 5:20, "Unless your *justice* exceeds that of the scribes and Pharisees, you will never enter the kingdom of heaven," and further on in Matthew 6:33, "but strive first for the kingdom of God and *God's justice*."

This is a hugely important point because many of us are used to interpreting *righteousness* in a purely personal way. As we fail to see the breadth of the challenge of *justice*, we are missing the message at the heart of the gospel. Seeking God's justice and living the way of God's justice is what the Christian community and the Christian way is all about.

THEOLOGY THAT LISTENS

I first heard the term *folk theologian* at the Dalit Resource Centre at Tamil Nadu Theological Seminary in Madurai, India. Dalits are those formerly called "outcastes" and "untouchable" and have no social status. But these people have embraced the name "Dalit," which means the "crushed" or "oppressed." Over 750 million Dalits now struggle for equality, dignity and human rights. I rather like the term *folk theologian*. Often when we talk about theology, we are referring to it in an academic sense, and yet I believe there is a theology that is more grassroots, that is, the theology of "God with sleeves rolled up." It is the theology of action or praxis, theology that combines reflection and action lived and expressed in the life of the community.

This turns theology on its head: instead of being something we export from universities in the West, we now let theology express itself in the context where people live. So we hear from the poor and the marginalized, we hear the gospel through their words and lives, and there is something true to the incarnation of Christ in their situation.

The term *folk theologian* reminds us that our theology should not just be from books or an academic context, but also learned from people struggling with oppression. Faith or religion too can oppress. But it also has the ability to liberate—if it listens.

ALL HUMANS ARE EQUAL

A couple of years ago on Christmas Eve I was in India and stood at a Buddhist meditative center dedicated to Dr. B. R. Ambedkar. Ambedkar was a most significant player in Indian politics, a Dalit who rose up to become the chair of those who put together the Indian constitution. The center is opposite the Taj Mahal, over the Yamuna River. On the wall outside are the words that Ambedkar wrote to explain his reasons for conversion from Hinduism to Buddhism. It is couched in the shape of twenty-two oaths he took, and he starts off by saying, "By discarding my ancient religion which stood for inequality and oppression, today I am reborn. Buddhism is a true religion and I will lead a life guided by the three principles of knowledge, right path and compassion."

Ambedkar converted with hundreds of thousands of other so-called untouchables to get away from the Varna system within Hinduism, which described him as outcaste. It is very interesting to see how this shapes his oaths: "I believe all human beings are equal" (9th); "I shall endeavor to establish equality" (10th); "I shall be compassionate to all living beings and I shall nurture them with care" (13th); "I therefore reject my old religion Hinduism which is detrimental to the prosperity of human kind and which discriminates between man and man and which treats me as inferior" (19th). My guide, who translated for me, was a Hindu himself, and it was kind of him to keep translating.

Since these beliefs are also Christian, I wondered why Ambedkar didn't convert to Christianity. And the sad response is that the caste prejudice he was longing to be liberated from persisted among Christians. So deep is the impact of caste within Indian society that even some Christian churches reflect it. Moreover, for Ambedkar Christianity remains the religion of colonialism.

THE LIBERATING MESSAGE

One of my most precious memories is preaching outdoors in Gomathimuthupuram, a Dalit village in Tamil Nadu, India, and being translated by our Amos Trust partner there, Jacob Devadason. I was preaching the liberating message of the gospel and of the value of every human being. It sent a shiver down my spine when people interrupted me to check the verses I was quoting from the Bible, to look them up in their own Bibles, because of the affirming message of Christianity and of the Hebrew (Old Testament) prophets. They were checking to see if this was true. If I was right!

Jesus came preaching and living the kingdom of God. *Kingdom* is a hard word because it has both patriarchal and monarchical meanings that can have negative connotations, and sometimes it helps us understand it better if we move away from the word *kingdom* and perhaps think of the *community* of God, a community that is underpinned not only by the lifestyle of Jesus but also by the teachings of Jesus and especially the teachings of the Sermon on the Mount. But "community of God" loses the political emphasis of the "kingdom of God," a deliberate use of words by Jesus that go up against the rulers of the time. *Kingdom* of God challenges rulers, dictators, empires and kingdoms because it is suggesting a style of community and a style of values that brings a revolutionary difference, a way of making community for the benefit of all. It is the kingdom/community of "love your neighbor as yourself" and "do to others as you would have them do to you," of those who acknowledge that "those who take the sword will perish by the sword."

One of the problems of sharing the gospel message is the church too often embraces the "Constantinian Compromise" (the compromise that the church makes to become acceptable to the empire—in the first case the Roman Empire). It is nice to be liked, to be acceptable within a community. It is attractive to be accepted by those in power, but we must never lose our prophetic role. We must "endeavor to establish equality" (quoting the tenth oath of Ambedkar)—our call is to speak truth to power. We must never lose the double-edged sword of the gospel or the power of God's revolution of love, which is a direct challenge to the way of empire.

Beware of Balance

The words *justice* and *peace* often go together, but sometimes people try to reach peace before there is justice, or even reconciliation before there is justice. The temptation to be "even-handed" or "balanced" is another danger. These terms are used when we would prefer to endorse the status quo. Isaiah 40:4 instructs us about bringing justice:

Every valley shall be lifted up,
    and every mountain and hill be made low;
the uneven ground shall become level,
    and the rough places a plain.

Injustice is badly imbalanced, and so unless we lift up those who are oppressed, dominated and forgotten, and challenge those who are dominating, there will be no equality or justice. There has to be a change of balance—a change of power. I am reminded of the words often attributed to Martin Luther King Jr., "No one is free until all are free," and this is why the struggle for justice is so worthwhile.

No Day of Vengeance of Our God

Luke's Gospel reveals something important about the attitude of God in Jesus' character. When Jesus first talks about his ministry in Nazareth (Luke 4:18-19), he says,

The Spirit of the Lord is upon me,
    because he has anointed me
        to bring good news to the poor.
He has sent me to proclaim release to the captives
    and recovery of sight to the blind,
        to let the oppressed go free,
to proclaim the year of the Lord's favor.

Jesus is quoting here from Isaiah 61:1-2. It is a very close quote, except he leaves out the words about "the day of vengeance of our God," which is interesting. The theology that becomes a reality in Bethlehem, the revolution that comes to Bethlehem, is not a revolution of vengeance but one that seems to suggest that a permanent year of jubilee—"the year of the Lord's favor"—will come when justice is brought to people.

So Jesus sees himself as bringing a revolution of justice, as was foreseen in Isaiah 9:6:

For a child has been born for us,
  a son given to us;
authority rests upon his shoulders;
  and he is named
Wonderful Counselor, Mighty God,
  Everlasting Father, Prince of Peace.

We often forget when we think about the birth of Jesus that he was soon a refugee, his family fleeing for their lives. We live in a world where because of the imbalance of resources people often have to flee, either for economic reasons or because of conflict. And yet many times people are not welcomed by communities that have more resources. But "God with us," whom we meet in the Bethlehem story, is God of the refugee, God of the asylum seeker, God of the oppressed, God of the poor and God of nonviolence—God of a revolution of love.

In Colossians 3:12-17 we are challenged to clothe ourselves with "compassion, kindness, humility, meekness and patience," to "bear with one another," to forgive, and "above all to clothe ourselves with love, which binds everything together in perfect harmony. And let the peace of Christ rule in our hearts" and with gratitude "sing psalms, hymns, and spiritual songs to God." These words are much tougher to do than they might appear. They are powerful and even painful words. What does it mean to be humble and meek, and to have the patience that will change this world? What does it mean to let the peace of Christ rule in our hearts? What does it mean to clothe ourselves with love?

At the very least it means to embrace and live by the words that echo from the beginning of the Bible: that every human being is made in the "image of God"—we are all equal—in Christ the barriers come down. It means journeying the way of Jesus, which we see reflected in Colossians 3 and also in the Sermon on the Mount.

The wonderful challenge of the Sermon on the Mount and Colossians 3 is to be peacemakers, to bring wholeness into a broken and unjust community, to echo the prophets of old, to do justice, to show mercy and walk humbly with God. Humility itself is so important because it refuses to dominate, it refuses to colonize, it sees everyone through the eyes of God. When we fail to do that we deny the gospel. We deny the tremendous message of the incarnation, which started in such a humble but powerful way in Bethlehem; in the end people will not walk our way unless they see the power of this humble, just faith—a faith that includes everyone and treats everyone equally.

We are called to be a community that brings down the mountains of oppression and lifts up the valleys of justice and righteousness so the pathways are made straight—as Martin Luther King Jr. was so fond of quoting from Isaiah 40:4.

Micah 6:8 talks of doing justice, showing mercy and walking humbly with God—this relates to the passage in Colossians 3, where we are called to clothe ourselves with compassion, to bear with one another, to forgive, and above all to clothe ourselves with love. This is the lifestyle of justice—a lifestyle of mercy, peacemaking and loving our neighbor as ourself.

HE BROKE THE RULES . . . AND BROUGHT THE REVOLUTION

What a wonderful moment when Jesus
reached through the divisions that hold people back.

Jesus affirmed the woman at the well in
a world that would not treat women as equal;

He touched the "untouchable"—reached out to the outcast,

broke through the barriers of racism, of
class, of gender and of caste.

This prophet was the great rule breaker.

He broke the rules that bind people and hold them back.

May we courageously follow this example
and exclude no one and welcome all.
May our churches be communities that
welcome all and may we understand the
deep joy of a gospel that nails our
prejudices and human divisions to a cross of shame

and awakens us to a resurrection of
community, love, equality and joy.

QUESTIONS FOR REFLECTION AND DISCUSSION

1. If you were asked what you think "God's calling card" would look like, what would you say? In what ways is "justice" a better answer?

2. In what ways can faith or religion oppress? How can it liberate in a practical way?

3. What are the implications of saying that the word "righteousness" would be better translated "justice"?

4. What does the author mean when he says, "It is nice to be liked, to be acceptable within a community. It is attractive to be accepted by those in power, but we must never lose our prophetic role." What danger is he warning the church or Christians about?

5. The author says, "We are all equal—in Christ the barriers come down." What barriers come down because of Christ?

6. Do you find it challenging to realize that theology has been "something we export from universities in the West" rather than letting "theology express itself in the context where people live"—even though most of the world's Christians are not within a Western culture? What do you think this means? What can Western Christians learn from other cultures?

2

BETHLEHEM IS CALLING

BETHLEHEM IS CALLING

Bethlehem is calling quietly—through the season's noise
Whispering of a conspiracy of love
Here it comes the news of love
The birth of God's new way of love
Breaking through the darkness bringing light

Here it comes from Bethlehem
So bow down low—start again
As a humble generous God
Stops to show us the way of love—from Bethlehem

Bethlehem is calling quietly—brings a gift of peace
Whispering of a conspiracy of love
To a world of wars and violence
This loving call's the one to heal us
Beat the swords to ploughshares—start again

Bethlehem is calling quietly—if you're still you'll hear
Whispering of a conspiracy of love
Breaking through to make you whole
A touch of love to heal the soul
The humble way of God bringing the light

CHORUS
Here it comes from Bethlehem
So bow down low—start again

As a humble generous God
Stops to show us the way of love—from Bethlehem

BETHLEHEM THEOLOGY

From the heart of Bethlehem, from the heart of occupied land, comes a theology to shake the world—a theology of hope, peace and justice.

So what is this Bethlehem theology? The style of the birth of Jesus in Bethlehem gives so many clues as to the character and nature of God. When God touches the earth, when it is the great moment of "God with us," a child is born in simplicity among a poor community. The wise men go looking for this remarkable event by talking to the local politician of power. But this is not where God is to be found. This is why this theology turns upside down the values of our world. Because instead of coming in status and power, the birth of the Prince of Peace is in vulnerability and humility. And soon Mary and Joseph and Jesus are fleeing as refugees to find safety in Africa. So these are the huge clues that show us that God is the God with the poor, the marginalized, those for whom there is no room—and this is why Bethlehem theology gives such hope, because no one is forgotten. The message is for all and the call is to build a community that makes all of this visible and tangible in our own generation.

At the time of Jesus' birth, Bethlehem was occupied territory—occupied by a powerful empire. But from both the lifestyle and message of the Prince of Peace came an alternative way that challenged empire. Empire was dominant, but Jesus revealed another way, which he expressed in the highly political phrase *the kingdom of God*. This challenge to the Roman Empire continues to challenge all empires; it also challenges us to model a community of justice and peace.

Looking at Bethlehem today we find the same message reflected and witnessed to. In Bethlehem there are those who continue to model "kingdom of God" as they stand up to the power of empire. They model what a community of justice looks like as they face the forces of domination with the light and lifestyle of the gospel.

The very style of the birth of Jesus in Bethlehem has significance for our understanding of the message of Christianity and its relevance to today's society. It is the moment when God touches earth and humanity and makes visible "God with us." Today, people are disregarded unless they have economic value. Though they may be involved in meaningful activities within the community, if they are not employed they are deemed "economically inactive." The birth of Jesus in simplicity and humility asserts the worth of every human being; God identifies with the poor and oppressed. The current view that selfishness is good and self-sacrifice is bad is a contradiction of what I call the "Bethlehem theology," which is visible in the birth of the Prince of Peace.

About three years ago at Christmas I received a Christmas card from Bishop Riah Hanna Abu el-Assal (the previous Anglican Bishop of Jerusalem). In it he referred to the birth of Jesus at Bethlehem as "a conspiracy of love." It is a beautiful phrase, almost reminiscent of "How silently, how silently" (from "O Little Town of Bethlehem"), that encapsulates the idea of something happening almost secretly. And this remarkable moment in time, which creeps in nearly unnoticed, reflects the deep love of God. Perhaps it is a conspiracy of the Trinity! The phrase *conspiracy of love* became part of the song "Bethlehem Is Calling."

I wrote "Bethlehem Is Calling" on Christmas day in church in Delhi, India. The worship group played some old carols beautifully and then transitioned to some modern worship songs that conveyed a message about "a mighty God" who dominates. I thought the older carols said it better, and I wanted to write a song that carried the theology of the birth in Bethlehem. We discover a humble, generous, loving God reaching out to all, including all, and this is the clue to our response.

To get into the Church of the Nativity in Manger Square in Bethlehem, we have to bow down because the entrance is so small. (It was adjusted like this to stop people riding in on horseback.) Somehow this sums up what our approach should be as we come to the birthplace of Christ. We are to approach it with humility, which reflects the way of God and the way of Jesus. It is an encounter that encourages us to start again, to be renewed.

How We Treat the Least

Michael Moore's documentary films are always entertaining. Whether you agree with the politics or not, they are powerful and relevant, even prophetic. His 2009 documentary *Capitalism: A Love Story* surprised me; it is an exposé of how capitalism without regulation reflects greed and exploitation. It points out that wherever capitalism has spread, it trumps democracy and allows the wealthy and powerful to get away with anything.

But the biggest surprise for me was where Moore goes to find values that critique what's happening in our society: his church. He interviews his priests and talks about his own motivations.

When I was a kid I wanted to be a priest. . . . It was because of the priests who went on the march to Selma [civil rights], or tried to stop the war [in Vietnam], or devoted their lives to the poor. They told me quite clearly what Jesus said, that the first shall be last and the last shall be first. That the rich man will have a very hard time getting into heaven, that we will be judged by how we treat the least among us, and that there are no people more important to God than the poor.

> Since that time, it seems that Jesus got hijacked by a lot of
> people who believe that the Son of God was sent here to
> create Heaven on Earth for the well-to-do. I must have
> missed that part of the Bible where Jesus became a capi-
> talist. . . . The rich have claimed [Jesus] for their very own.[1]

Moore contrasts the way of Jesus with the love of money reflected on Wall Street—he quotes Senator Bernie Sanders from
Vermont who said, "Wall Street became very religious in wor-
shiping greed." In the special features on the DVD Moore has a
chat with Father Dick Preston, his priest. Moore comments, "If
people just followed the basic teachings of Jesus it seems like the
planet would be a lot better off." Father Preston says, "What
drew all the people to Jesus was his sense that God was with him
and his insistence that all had a right to life, to justice and mercy
and that all had a right to be present at the table." This is a clear
understanding of Bethlehem theology and how it is made visible.

In contrast to our own Western societies, where the division
between the rich and the poor is so great and getting greater,
Bethlehem theology instructs us on how we should live and how
we should try to structure society in these circumstances. There
is something wrong when the power, resources and money are
in the hands of 1 percent of the community. Society has lost its
commitment to community, to the common good and to justice.

The obsession with the love of money, the handing over so
much power and significance and even moral arguments to
economists, means we are losing many key aspects of humanity
and certainly something of the value of every human being.

The foundational Bible teaching that all are made in the image
of God remains a challenge to the world where 1 percent own so
much. Bailing out banks too large to fail and their bankers, who
earn more than ordinary people can even imagine, was strange,

especially as austerity is being imposed on society and it is affecting the less-well-off more than the wealthy.

We've got very uneven situations between the rich and the poor in our world. One example that occurred in my own country was a banker who complained that he was only getting a £4 million bonus while a friend of his at another bank was getting a £6 million bonus—he was furious. And meanwhile those who have less, the poor of our country, are being made to live in austerity to cope with the mess the bankers have made. Nobody needs that kind of money; we have arrived at a point in history where we can't afford the rich.

The Occupy movements that sprang up around the world raised these issues. In London an attempt to camp outside the Stock Exchange was unsuccessful, so Occupiers camped right outside St. Paul's Cathedral instead. As I wandered around the camp and listened to what was being said, I recognized attitudes that tied in well with our biblical principles of caring equally for all people. Bethlehem theology points out that when God touches earth and gives us a clear picture of the values and attitude of God, it reveals God's identification with the humble, the poor and the refugees. This is not a god of status, power and the 1 percent. God is not hierarchical or dictatorial, but is instead generous and brings a revolution of love.

BETHLEHEM TODAY

In Bethlehem today we find the same witness of Jesus being carried on. Two of Amos Trust's partners in Bethlehem are Wi'am Conflict Resolution Centre and Holy Land Trust. Wi'am is based in a beautiful, old Palestinian house right beside the huge separation wall. This devastating separation wall, which the International Court of Justice has said must come down, conveys the message that the people living in this community are not wanted; this community must be invisible; it is a community to be warehoused and ignored. Had the wall been built on the green line (the pre-1967 border), then maybe we could accept the view that it is for security. However, it weaves in and out of the West Bank, taking land and cutting off communities from one another.

A garden has been planted by the wall in Bethlehem. Right beside the twenty-five-foot separation wall are beautiful trees and plants. These trees and plants and the people there reflect eternal truths and eternal justice. They will outlast the wall. Here people pursue reconciliation, receive counseling, pause and draw strength as they walk in the garden—right next to the huge, overshadowing, gray wall. This is the work of Wi'am.

Places of beauty can be made in surprising places, and there a witness can happen that somehow makes the domination and the imprisonment look ridiculous. Zoughbi Zoughbi is director of Wi'am, and after enouraging me to plant a tree, he gave me a T-shirt with a picture of the wall and the trees they are planting. The roots of these trees have somehow grown under the wall, and great cracks have appeared, so the wall is coming down. The writing on the T-shirt says, "No injustice will last forever."

These people bring hope to young and old. They show the outworking of the Bethlehem theology of love, which reaches out to all. Even though 87 percent of Bethlehem's traditional land has been taken, some residents still refuse to give up on the possibility of good news, the possibility of peace on earth. They refuse to give up. In the end the values they witness to—justice, right living and care for the community—will outlive the values of oppression, domination, greed and racism.

The witness of the garden by the wall is a parable for us all: you can imprison people, you can take away their land, and you can take away their homes, but you can't take away their spirit—

you can't take away their hope in a gospel of liberation. In a very special way hope was born centuries ago in Bethlehem; it is still born anew today in the lives of people who witness and light candles and plant trees against all odds. This is Bethlehem theology in action, which brings hope for all.

Down the road at Holy Land Trust, executive director Sami Awad and his team are training people in nonviolent resistance. It is essential, they believe, that nonviolence should become the dominant way to resist the occupation and the Israeli settlements. And though the nonviolence is often met with considerable violence by the Israeli army, the Holy Land Trust asserts that there is no hope in a violent response. They point out that they are following the ways of Martin Luther King Jr. and Mahatma Gandhi, but also the way of Jesus, who said, "all who take the sword will perish by the sword" (Matthew 26:52). So the witness of the Prince of Peace continues in Bethlehem through many who are also responding nonviolently and showing hope in a place where you might feel there is no hope.

It is sometimes hard, particularly at Christmas time, to remember how revolutionary Jesus' birth in Bethlehem was. It is a highly significant lesson about God's commitment to humans, the identification with the poor, the vulnerable, the forgotten, the homeless and the refugees. It is a powerful message on how Christians should live, how we should be motivated by our encounter with God. It is rooted in the Hebrew prophets. Jesus quotes from Isaiah to define his own ministry in Luke 4:18-19. He speaks in terms of setting free the oppressed, releasing the captives and bringing good news to the poor. When the Christian community does this, not only is justice visible but so is Jesus.

The style of Jesus' birth in Bethlehem says to the forgotten, ignored, homeless and oppressed, "You are valued. You are treated as if you are nobody, but in fact you are somebody."

When God became human in Jesus, God was not identifying with those of status and power, but with the mistreated and forgotten, and this is the affirming, liberating, inclusive, joyful power of the gospel.

I often say, "Bethlehem is for life and not just for Christmas." In our churches we come to Bethlehem once a year in Advent and Christmas, but we can forget that the coming of the Prince of Peace is for the whole year. We also forget that the community of God in Bethlehem are living, witnessing, resisting and being faithful to God throughout the year. We need to remember them throughout the year and give them support in their struggle.

Establish Justice in the Gate

One day I was on the hills around Bethlehem visiting a family whose home had just been demolished by the Israeli army. The army had come early in the morning, and with virtually no warning the family was given a few minutes to grab any possessions they could and then told to get out. A huge bulldozer plowed into their home and destroyed it. It was winter, and the people were sitting in a tent beside their demolished home. Looking around I saw a little village not far away and asked the name of the village. They said it is Tekoa. And I realized this was the area where the prophet Amos had come from. I remembered his words "let justice roll down like waters, and right living like an ever-flowing stream" (Amos 5:24), and how once again in this area these words needed to be heard.

Amos is a dramatic book with the prophet criticizing first Israel's neighbors when they failed to be just and even committed war crimes in order to gain more territory (see Amos 1:13, for example). And so it goes on, and if we imagine him speaking to the people of Israel, then it was probably acceptable to hear their neighbors being critiqued.

But when we get to Amos 2:6-7 Israel is criticized. It must have been a powerful moment,

because they sell the just for silver
and the needy for a pair of sandals—
they who trample the head of the poor into the dust of
the earth,
and push the afflicted out of the way.

This is uncomfortable because it hits so close to home, and Amos goes on, "[they] commanded the prophets, saying, 'You shall not prophesy'" (v. 12). He is referring to those "that turn justice to wormwood, and bring righteousness to the ground" (Amos 5:7). The challenge is for them to seek the Lord and live (Amos 5:4). Justice is at the heart of what God loves. In Amos 5:15 he says, "Hate evil and love good, and establish justice in the gate." Then come these remarkable words:

I despise your festivals,
and I take no delight in your solemn assemblies.
Even though you offer me your burnt offerings and grain
offerings,
I will not accept them;
and the offerings of well-being of your fatted animals
I will not look upon.
Take away from me the noise of your songs;
I will not listen to the melody of your harps.
But let justice roll down like waters,
and righteousness like an ever-flowing stream.
(Amos 5:21-24)

Amos Trust was founded by a musician, therefore it is particularly interesting to see verse 23, which is the only place in the Bible where music is criticized, and it is criticized because people are not caring for the poor and are not living out the justice of God while they play their music. Amos 8:3-6 says,

"The songs of the temple shall become wailings in that day,"
    says the Lord GOD. . . .
Hear this, you that trample on the needy,
    and bring to ruin the poor of the land,
saying, "When will the new moon be over
    so that we may sell grain;
and the sabbath,
    so that we may offer wheat for sale?
We will make the ephah small and the shekel great,
    and practice deceit with false balances,
buying the poor for silver
    and the needy for a pair of sandals,
    and selling the sweepings of the wheat."

Amos is pointing out that this corruption is not acceptable to God. And then in verse 10, "I will turn your feasts into mourning, and all your songs into lamentation." So don't sing your songs of worship and ignore justice.

Throughout Amos, the prophet says God is calling people to take note of the needs of the poor and to work for justice. This is part of the heritage of the Bethlehem area, and these words have relevance to our own communities, where the division between rich and poor is tearing society apart. It is better for all if there is a community of equality, which brings justice to all.

The prophet Amos is dedicated to justice. Theologian and Amos partner Reverend Jasmine Devadason from Gomathimuthupuram, Tamil Nadu, India, develops this point and shows its relevance to today's world:

Amos connects justice with life—where Israel does not practice justice, the community declines. To have life in the community, justice and righteousness must roll down like a river after the winter rains and persevere like those few streams that remain the same even during the summer drought. For Amos justice is not an abstract concept but it is a life giving power. So the importance of justice is a main thrust in the book of Amos which is relevant for today's context.

Trading/marketing had become the major part of the life of the rich. The rich businessmen of the day were saying, "When will the New Moon be over that we may sell grain, and the Sabbath be ended that we may market wheat?" verse 5a, so that they could gain wealth by exploiting the poor.

A similar situation exists today. Although the global economy as a whole has grown over the last 20 years, the economies of many poor countries have actually shrunk. While their share of world trade is tiny, trade for individual poor countries is actually a far more significant contributor to their national income than for most rich countries. Nearly a third of Africa's income is accounted for by trade— a much higher proportion than for Europe or the USA. This means that the impact of international trade rules and policies tends to be far greater on poor countries than rich countries. International trade today does not work for the poor but it could play an important role, if paid fairly, which can offer people living in poverty the dignity of a just reward for their labor. However, the reality of mainstream trade is that it is rife with exploitation.[2]

So what does it mean to "let justice roll" in Amos's hometown and land today? Pastor Mitri Raheb of Evangelical Lutheran

Christmas Church in Bethlehem says, "Christians in Palestine are forced to ask themselves what God's justice means to a people whose members suffer under systematic political, social, and economic injustice. What does 'freedom in Christ' mean to people living under occupation and denied basic rights? What does the cross mean to a people constantly crucified and marked by suffering?"[3]

This powerful quote rings true to what Jesus says in Matthew 6:33: we should "strive first for the kingdom of God and his justice." When we find a situation where God's justice is being ignored and people are suffering, we have a responsibility to act. Particularly when those people and their Christian community have called out to us to listen and to respond with justice to their needs. We have to be part of a revolution of hope that begins by listening to those who are oppressed and particularly listening to their prophets—for instance those who have written the Kairos Palestine document (see chap. 4). No more "silencing of the prophets."

WHY NONVIOLENCE?

This aspect of Bethlehem theology is still practiced in Bethlehem today as a way of combating the power of empire. Sami Awad is dedicated to nonviolence because, as he says,

> it addresses key issues of the conflict that are vital in helping it move into a place where resolution and peace become possible.
>
> It gives an opportunity for every member of a community to be involved, no matter how old they are and what their status is in society. Everyone can choose to play a role that best fits their desires and commitment—from participating in the street protests, to engaging in simply

boycotting the products of the oppressor in the household.

Armed resistance does not only limit who participates in the resistance (i.e., groups of mostly young men who have a certain physical and mental capacity to engage in such actions); it strongly discourages those who want to participate in nonviolent protests from engaging due to the likelihood that the system of oppression will justify its attacks even on nonviolent protests claiming that even such protests harbor violent agents in them.

Nonviolence . . . seeks to break the cycle of violence between the conflicting factions. This may not happen immediately and it is actually more likely that the oppressor will try to engage in suppressing the nonviolent protests violently in its initial stages. But once it is able to grow and mobilize a greater number of the community—and more importantly a greater number of the community that belongs to the suppressor—then a shift occurs. Now many of those who were directly engaging in the suppression begin to morally and emotionally lose connection with the justification of why they have to engage in violence to suppress the other.

A final value of nonviolence is that it provides an opportunity for healing of both the oppressor and the oppressed. In regards to the oppressed, nonviolence empowers a community to stand up for its rights and seek its justice.

The worst expression of oppression is when a community victimizes itself to the oppression and accepts resignation and hopelessness; nonviolence seeks to break that condition. . . . Once the oppressed engage in nonviolence— not seeking to physically, emotionally, or spiritually inflict pain on the other—and the other begins to see this, then the oppressor can no longer justify their action towards the other, locally and globally.[4]

One time when I was in the Holy Land Trust office in Bethlehem Sami gave me a poster with words by Martin Luther King Jr. that speak with great power and resonance and support his view:

The ultimate weakness of violence is that it is a descending spiral begetting the very thing it seeks to destroy. Instead of diminishing evil, it multiplies it. Through violence you may murder the liar, but you cannot murder the lie, nor establish the truth. Through violence you murder the hater, but you do not murder hate. In fact, violence merely increases hate. Returning violence for violence multiplies violence, adding deeper darkness to a night already devoid of stars. Darkness cannot drive out darkness; only light can do that. Hate cannot drive out hate; only love can do that.[5]

THE GREAT PERIL OF THE DEADENING OF CONSCIENCE

I was making a film in Bethlehem (*Bethlehem Hidden from View*) and standing by the separation wall, which surrounds most of Bethlehem, with Jewish Israeli academic and activist Jeff Halper. I was struck as he talked about the "warehousing" of the Palestinian people. Though Jeff says he is not a religious person and calls himself a secular Jew, he said, "If this is not a theological issue then what is?" He put his finger on a point right at the heart of our theology—if all humans are made in the image of God and we see some treated as less than others, it goes against the message and lifestyle of hope that was made visible in Bethlehem, because warehousing a community is a way of dismissing them, of saying, "You are of no value."

If our theology and spirituality are only for ourselves, if they take us away from what's happening in the world, then they are not of the Bethlehem theology expressed so clearly in the birth of Jesus. Bethlehem theology makes God visible in the poverty, struggles and oppression of our world.

I've been reading Thomas Merton's *Book of Hours*, which has a little passage to read at different times of day, each day of the week. Merton (who was a Trappist monk, poet and social activist) says, "the great danger is that under the pressures of anxiety and fear the people of the world will come to accept gradually the idea of war, the idea of submission to total power, and the abdication of reason, spirit and individual conscience. The great peril is the deadening of conscience."[6] This is the great peril—because dead consciences reject the kingdom/community of God.

So we need a spirituality that keeps our consciences alive and listens to the call of those suffering oppression, while rejecting war and violence as a solution. We need a spirituality that rises higher than walls and beyond checkpoints, that reaches to ignored children and forgotten people wherever they may be, that reaches beyond fear and toward hope, that does unto others as we would want them to do to us. In journeying this way we "let justice roll."

As we weigh the importance of the birth of Jesus, particularly in our Advent and Christmas events, we often quote from Isaiah 9:6, which says, "For a child has been born for us, . . . and he is named . . . Prince of Peace." Christians look at this passage from the Hebrew Scriptures and feel that it sums up something highly significant about the birth of Jesus. God touching the earth in this extraordinary way gives a depth of insight into the character of God, the style of God and the bias of God. What is the significance of the title Prince of Peace? It is a title of the kingdom/community of God. This alternative community does not dominate by power and violence—its leadership is dedicated to peacemaking.

In the early days of Christianity it was accepted that the Christian way was nonviolent. But when the church made a deal with empire in the days of Constantine, it began to embrace violence and later blessed and even encouraged violence, like during the Crusades, which were a horrendous denial of what the gospel is about.

But this still goes on today—we live in countries that espouse violence and try to maintain peace by domination and the use of violence. But *we* call anyone who uses violence in response to us "terrorists." Yet the gospel says no to the violence and domination of empire. And Jesus' Palm Sunday entrance into Jerusalem (gentle and on a donkey—the opposite of empire's way of entering the city) says no to violence. Empire uses violence, but it is not the way of God. The kingdom/community of God, which Jesus talked about so much, has different values from empire, values that challenge all domination and power (see chap. 5).

BETHLEHEM IS CALLING

Many from Bethlehem speak words that reflect the Bethlehem theology, but I have chosen to introduce you to three friends and partners from whom we have seen the light and the theology of Bethlehem coming alive in action. They help to make the way of Jesus visible, and their words make us hear Bethlehem calling. We will be strengthened by listening to them.

First, Dr. Mazin Qumsiyeh, a doctor of biology and medical genetics, is an activist, peace builder and Christian from Beit Sahour (the Shepherd's Fields area). He speaks the Bethlehem message to the world.

Jesus was born here—he was the prince of peace. Islam also recognizes him as a prophet and prince of peace, as someone who promotes peace in the world, who tries to repair humanity, so this is the message that started here.

We Palestinian Muslims and Christians believe it is a message not just for us individuals here in this area, but it is a message for all humanity. It is a message of humanity, a message of justice and peace and a message of light against darkness, a message of hope and empowerment. So, for example, I was born in Beit Sahour, the Shepherd's Fields. I talk passionately about this subject—those shepherds two thousand years ago saw the star, they went up to Bethlehem to see what was going on, and then . . . it was not just that they were supposed to see, they were supposed to go and tell—to go and tell the truth to others, and to go and effect the change.

So we believe in the message of Jesus and the message that was delivered that day two thousand years ago—that we have a mission in life. Our life is not just to sit around and eat and drink and get married and be happy and go to church and pray; all of this is good and fine, but if we do not fulfill this mission that was given to us then we are really derelict in our duties. What is the Bethlehem message to the world? There is the star with the light coming from it. It is a message of challenging the forces of darkness, challenging the evil that is in this world, and challenging it in a spirit of humility, with love for others, respect for others and their opinions, and not in the hateful mode of killing another human being; it is a message of love, not a message of hate.

At the time Jesus was here, walking around these places, there was a lot of injustice, there was a lot of disease, there was a lot of inhumanity, humans treating fellow humans with lack of dignity, lack of respect—and Jesus chose to be among the people who are oppressed. He could have chosen not to do that—but he chose to associate with the poorest, with the most oppressed people on earth, and to work with them, to liberate them, to empower them, to strengthen them.

So follow the example of Jesus who said—leave all your belongings, all your wealth, that is not how you get into heaven; it is actually more difficult for the rich man to enter heaven than it is for a camel to pass through the eye of a needle. These are the messages that Jesus taught.[7]

Second, Zoughbi Zoughbi relates the Christmas story to the experience of Wi'am Conflict Resolution Centre, Bethlehem.

Christ's miraculous birth was that critical first step toward a new positive change for the whole world. Following Jesus' footsteps, we at Wi'am embark on transformation on a personal and community level. Our lord Jesus challenged the system and was able to change it through agape, perseverance, and enticement of collective responsibility. In the Spirit of Christ we are asking for our rights while we continue to invest in unity. Thus, we struggle for rights with unity, as Jesus did long ago.

We know that Christ, without raising a sword, aroused the lethal anger of both the occupier and its collaborators. He spoke the truth fearlessly to the powers and we are proud to live where he was born and remember him as a native son of our land. We would be remiss to forget the commitment of Mary and Joseph, who were forced by Roman Occupation to come here for the census. But also fled with the child into Egypt to save his life. Many steps remained in his journey, as in ours. The work of mending our nation, and our world, is continuous. *We pray that all nations . . . will find the embracing arms of dialogue open and stand against the ongoing dialogue of arms.* Those who would use weapons to bully as well as those who would make and sell them for profit are reversing our global peace process. We believe the diplomatic struggle is part of the nonviolent path, asserting our rights with words on the national and international stages.[8]

Third, Sami also spoke on the message of Bethlehem:

The birth of Christ in Bethlehem is very important because it is a message of creating a new future and it is a message of healing. Jesus came to Bethlehem, he was born in Bethlehem and he came at a very important, pivotal point to give a message of peace. His message was about us moving into a new domain, into a new paradigm, a new reality that we need to engage in by following his teachings.

Jesus . . . did not come and simply attack the past history; he honored the history, he respected the history of the Jewish community, he understood the laws, he followed the laws but he said that we should move forward. We must not allow our future to be completely ruled by the laws of the past, by the habits and traditions of the past. . . . I think Bethlehem stands at this pivotal point today. Bethlehem is the place that can really represent this message.

We need to create a new reality in the Holy Land, a new structure where every person that lives here—that was born here, Israeli, Palestinian, Jew, Christian and Muslim, is honored for who they are so their history and their past is respected. We need to create a new future together, a new reality, a new kingdom as Jesus would say for this holy land to become a real light amongst all nations.

At the moment Bethlehem is surrounded by a wall—it looks ignored and the sad reality is that people don't know about it. The international community, Christians in the

West, cannot comprehend the fact, even when we tell them that Bethlehem is surrounded by walls and fences and there are only three ways to go in and out and we are completely controlled by Israeli military check points they cannot understand that. People need to come and then be witnesses to this, and then they need to go and speak.[9]

So as these witnesses have shown us, faith, justice, hope and dignity are alive and well in Bethlehem today amid the struggle for justice. The light of hope is still visible in the suffering, and that calls for a response from us.

IN TIMES LIKE THESE

Lord, in times like these how should I live?
Show me the path of peacemaking.
I bring my prejudices to you
And ask that you will continue to convert me
Day by day and step by step on the way
So that I never build up walls of division
But become one of those who show that
In Christ these divisions are finished.
Lord, may I be a child of God
Walking steadily on the path of peacemaking.
And will you feed my soul, nourish my spirit and lift me up?
In times like these how should I live?

QUESTIONS FOR REFLECTION AND DISCUSSION

1. How do you understand the "'Bethlehem theology,' which is visible in the birth of the Prince of Peace"?

2. The author states that the birth of Jesus in Bethlehem "pro-

vides a powerful message on how Christians should live."
How would you sum up this message?

3. Do you think the society you live in "has lost its commitment
to community, to the common good and to justice"? Explain
your answer.

4. Dr. Mazin Qumsiyeh said, "At the time Jesus was here,
walking around these places, there was a lot of injustice,
there was a lot of disease, there was a lot of inhumanity,
humans treating fellow humans with lack of dignity, lack of
respect—and Jesus chose to be among the people who are
oppressed. . . . [H]e chose to associate with the poorest, with
the most oppressed people on earth, and to work with them,
to liberate them, to empower them, to strengthen them. So
follow the example of Jesus." Think about your own society
or situation—what does following Jesus' example mean
where you are?

5. The author says, "If our theology and spirituality are only for
ourselves, if they take us away from what's happening in the
world, then they are not of the Bethlehem theology expressed
so clearly in the birth of Jesus." Is this true? How might an
understanding of theology and spirituality take us away from
what's happening in the world?

BE THE HANDS OF JESUS
The Community of Love

COMMUNITY OF LOVE

She rediscovered her religion in St Joseph's of the Mountain
In the little Episcopal church in the Honduran town
Of San Pedro Sula when she joined the congregation
And drew strength from the Eucharist in a community of love

She turned on her TV, and she heard the Bishop speaking
After the 10 o'clock news and before the evening film
And he told her how God loved her just the way she was,
And she could come and join the family in a community of love.

She found strength in a community of love
She found love in a community of faith
She found faith in a community of God
She found God in a community of love

She was welcomed to the family of the carpenter from Nazareth
Where those who are forgotten find strength to start again
They find mercy and forgiveness and in linking arms together
They are lifted up to dignity in a community of love

She found strength in a community of love
She found love in a community of faith
She found faith in a community of God
She found God in a community of love

"Community of Love" was written after a visit to San Pedro Sula, Honduras. I had been invited by Leo Frade, the bishop of Honduras at that time, to do some concerts, mainly in schools. We also spent time visiting the churches of part of his diocese. The song reflects how each church was living out the gospel's values by caring for the needy and for the local community, and that this action goes hand in glove with the faith and the spirituality of the churches.

Soon after I wrote the song, Hurricane Mitch hit Honduras, specifically the area where we had been visiting. Mitch made a big impact. The churches took the lead in caring for those affected, and Bishop Leo wrote a very moving article, carried in the UK press, about the needs and how people were responding. This is what I would have expected of them, having seen that every church was doing practical things that made visible the justice and the concern of the gospel. I felt that the song I had given them had the right title—"A Community of Love." They were making the love and the attitude of Jesus visible in very tangible ways.

On another occasion I was in a little place called La Concepción about fifteen miles from Managua, Nicaragua. It is a community of tremendous poverty; a very high percentage of the people are unemployed. I was taken to the little Baptist church where I was asked to preach. Before we even got inside, the people had pulled some fruit from the trees in the churchyard to give me as a gift. As I looked around at them and the poverty of their small town I thought, *What shall I say?* I decided to speak on Jesus of Nazareth because Nazareth was not a significant place, maybe between eighty and two hundred people in the time of Jesus. It was so insignificant that Nathanael said of it, "Can any good come from Nazareth?" (Which, no doubt, was partly because he suffered from a complex, coming from Cana, which was even smaller.)

As I talked to the people about the insignificance of Nazareth, I began to stress the character of Jesus, who came from this little place, and what this told us about the character of God. I asked them if they had met Jesus of La Concepción, and everyone nodded—and they all got the point. They knew Jesus of La Concepción because they knew that Jesus of Nazareth identifies with those who are normally forgotten and passed by. He was not Jesus of Jerusalem, Jesus of Rome, Jesus of New York City or Jesus of London. He did not come from a place of power or during a time of mass communication. He was not Jesus the televangelist. He was Jesus of Nazareth. I have been to many places around the world where people say, "Can any good come from here?" It is a great comfort to those people to know that Jesus came from such a place.

Our Christian catechism and teaching tell us that Jesus is the second person of the Trinity—God the Father, God the Son and God the Holy Spirit. This is what the Christian church has believed and asserted through history: when Jesus was born, God touched the earth. In Jesus God walked among us and in some way can be known among us today. So as we look at Jesus, we should expect to learn about the character of God.

I remember trying to write an extra verse for an Iona Community song, "He Became Poor," to try to summarize the significance of Jesus, particularly the impact of his birth—his incarnation—when God became a human being. I wrote these words:

He became poor that we might discover our worth
He became flesh of our flesh to dignify our humanity
At the stable door our lives are changed and we bow in
humility
As we find God, utterly vulnerable, yet turning the world
upside down.

This is the significance of Jesus—our view of God is changed—
we see God not as domineering but as vulnerable, and we learn
about the values of God's reign.

M. Scott Peck says, "Christ is known as the Suffering Servant,
many think of Jesus therefore as passive, almost weak. . . . They
do not realize that when he washed the feet of those who called
him Lord, he began to overturn the entire social order as he
continues to overturn it today."[1] So we see Jesus as a serving,
suffering God, but also as living and present and radical or revolutionary. Let's look more closely at the way of Jesus and where
Bethlehem theology begins.

THE BIRTH OF JESUS

This story tells us that God becomes human as a vulnerable and
powerless baby born into humble circumstances. The an-
nouncement of the birth of Jesus is first delivered to shepherds,
who were considered to be the lowest of the low in the community. They were nobodies, and yet they were treated by God
as somebodies—the first to hear the good news.

While Luke has the shepherds, Matthew includes the wise
men. Maybe they are both symbolic—Luke sees the humble and
the poor as being the recipients of the message of the angels,
while Matthew sees the wisdom of the world bowing before this
vulnerable king who will turn kingship on its head by serving
others. Jesus is born at least in simplicity, probably poverty, possibly in a cave among the animals. Soon he is a refugee fleeing
to Egypt. There are all sorts of echoes of homelessness and
poverty, of refugees and asylum seekers here. So immediately at
the beginning of the Gospels Jesus, or we could say God, identifies with the weakest, the victims and the forgotten, and thereby
gives them value. Already this is good news.

In India I have visited the Dalits, people treated as nobodies.

Dalit is the word they have chosen to describe themselves; it means despised, ground down. I spent time in the villages hearing the stories of abuse and victimization firsthand. Then I went to the Dalit Liberation Theology Centre at Tamil Nadu Theological College and discovered that Jesus is their good news. They are delighted to say that the crushed, the broken, the oppressed find value in Dalit theology, which says, "No people become God's people. . . . In our suffering we find God. Our own experience of suffering unites us with this suffering God."[2] The people drummed and they danced for us to express their rebirth as human beings after the centuries of oppression.

So the style of the birth of Jesus is good news; it says that we all are valued.

THE LIFE OF JESUS

The life and teachings of Jesus also reveal much to us. He does not reject outcastes, whether they be lepers or tax collectors. He values and affirms women in a way that went against the culture of his day (e.g., the extraordinary discussion with the Samaritan woman at the well, in today's Nablus). Actually, clues are given right from the start in Matthew's genealogy. Included in the list are four fascinating women—Tamar, Rahab, Ruth and Bathsheba (referred to as the wife of Uriah). The genealogy also mentions Mary. What is Matthew saying? He is preparing us for the unorthodox birth of Jesus by introducing us to women who may have been treated without respect and yet reflect God's unusual work, which is also seen in God's choice of Mary to be the mother of Christ.

Tamar, who was probably not an Israelite, pretended to be a temple prostitute in order to sleep with her father-in-law, who hadn't kept his promise to her (Genesis 38). Rahab, the prostitute and also not an Israelite, gave shelter to the Israelites spying on Jericho (Joshua 2). She is seen as virtuous for this. Ruth was a Moabite, and Bathsheba, the wife of Uriah the Hittite, was probably a Hittite. The inclusiveness of this list is remarkable. Despite the fact that women were regularly left out of genealogies in those days, these women are included because they played a part in God's plan despite their unorthodox relationships and not being from the Jewish community. So Matthew is making the point that something about Mary too might have been unorthodox, but she fitted in happily with this genealogy. And so from the beginning of Matthew's Gospel the scene is being set to prepare people for the remarkable inclusiveness of Jesus.

Jesus has come to introduce God's reign and the values of God's community, the kingdom of God. And inclusivity is a key to it. He often talks about the kingdom as a banquet. Kenneth Bailey points out that though Isaiah speaks of Yahweh making a banquet for all people and for all nations (Isaiah 25:6-10), in the intertestamental period the inclusion of Gentiles in this banquet gets played down and Isaiah's vision is lost. In *1 Enoch* 62 the Gentiles suffer punishment and are driven out. In the Qumran community, from which the Dead Sea Scrolls originated, people come to meet the Messiah in ranks. "The Messianic Rule" teaches us that "First are the judges and officers: then come the chiefs of thousands, fifties and tens; finally, there are the Levites."[3] No one is allowed in who is "smitten in his flesh, or paralyzed in his feet or hands, or lame, or blind or deaf or dumb or smitten in his flesh with a visible blemish." All Gentiles are obviously excluded, and along with them all imperfect Jews, says Kenneth Bailey.[4] So Isaiah's great vision has been watered down. Enoch has excluded the Gentiles—and the Qumran community rejects the Jewish unrighteous and those with any physical blemish or disability.

Jesus' invitation is the exact opposite. In other words, bring in the poor, the crippled, the blind and the lame; or as Matthew puts it, "the last will be first, and the first will be last" (Matthew 20:16; see also Mark 10:31; Luke 13:30).

This, I believe, is symbolic of the Eucharist, the great banquet, the great equalizer, the inclusive and prophetic moment. We have sometimes made it a meal that divides, but I believe it was meant to be where *all* can kneel, draw strength and be refreshed and renewed. Here all can repent and find forgiveness.

From the beginning Jesus invited his listeners to repent— "Repent, and believe the good news" (Mark 1:15). Tom Wright points out that "in our world telling people to repent and believe is likely to be heard as a summons to give up personal sins and accept a body of dogma or a scheme of religious salvation."[5] This is a classic occasion where we have to unlearn our normal readings and allow the first century itself to tell us what to hear instead. The phrase "Repent, and believe the good news" actually means "give up your agendas and trust me for mine."[6] Wright points out that though there is a religious or spiritual dimension, we must not screen out the practical and political challenge that these words convey. Jesus' ministry is showing us God's agenda, the values of God's kingdom and how we should live as God's community. Jesus was a threat to the authorities because he challenged the order of things, including the temple itself. He broke open their control. And his Sermon on the Mount reminds us profoundly of the nature of the welcoming God.

On a couple of occasions I have been taken to the Mount of Beatitudes, where the Sermon on the Mount is traditionally held to have been given, by the Greek Melkite Palestinian Israeli priest Elias Chacour (now archbishop of Galilee). He is a remarkable peacemaker, and he has expounded the Sermon on the

Mount on this spot. He has committed his life to the way of peace and to introducing people to Jesus, whom he calls his champion. He works diligently for justice and peace for his own community—the Palestinian people—and also for reconciliation between Palestinians and Jews. As we sat on the Mount, he reminded us that this is a different mountain from the one on which the Ten Commandments were given. He says,

> compare what happened on Mount Horeb in the Sinai where no one was allowed even to touch the mountain. You needed to keep away, to keep afar. If you touched the mountain you were killed. Here if you don't come closer Jesus will call you, "Please come closer, you poor, you paralyzed, you sick man, you lady, come closer. I love you. I want to reveal to you one thing, that my Father loves you so much and he trusts you all so much. So this is the mountain of closeness as opposed to the mountain that says keep far off.[7]

This is the mountain of inclusiveness as opposed to the mountain of exclusiveness. So Jesus reveals to us the character of God that welcomes all, redeems and renews all, and then calls us to be a community—to go and create these circumstances.

Chacour also talks about the way the beatitudes are translated. For instance, "Blessed are the peacemakers": "Blessed" is sometimes translated as "Happy," which he says is the worst translation. He says in the Aramaic the word is active and means "go and do—go and create these circumstances." In fact he reads the beatitudes like this:

> Seeing the multitudes he went up onto a mountain and when he sat down his disciples came to him and he opened his mouth and taught them saying "Get up, go ahead, move,

do something. Yes, get your hands dirty, you poor in spirit, for yours is the Kingdom of Heaven. Get up, go ahead, do something. Get your hands dirty you hungry and thirsty for justice. Get up, go ahead, don't contemplate but get your hands dirty if you want to be peacemakers, peace-builders, peace-constructors, and not peace-contemplators. Do something about that."[8]

So Archbishop Elias Chacour is reminding us to be those who get up and do, to live out the values of God's community. To welcome women, foreigners, the marginalized, the outcast, children, the poor, any group that we would normally exclude, which Jesus would include.

Jesus is clarifying our picture of God, yet the temptation is to reflect a God who is tribal, primitive, brutal. Our faith easily can slip into this. It is faith—both Christian and Jewish—that tells the Palestinians they are insignificant and should get out of their land, just as Christians through the centuries have oppressed and killed Jews. The same happened to the Dalits; the caste system of Hinduism says that they are nothing, and faith itself is oppressing them. So faith must be liberated in our time.

I have been shaken by my visits to the Middle East, where I spent a lot of time interviewing people who have given up on faith because it harbors so much oppression. Many people committed to peace have found that religion causes oppression. This is exactly what Jesus was trying to cut through by saying we should not be exclusive. Don't say, "We are chosen, and you are not." Don't say, "This person can't enter the temple." We have to move beyond the tribal view of God. Jesus, through his example in his life and ministry, points to the God of wholeness, healing, peace and justice—he lives and challenges us to live good news.

THE DEATH OF JESUS

The events of the week leading to the death of Jesus—Holy Week—are hugely significant signs.

First, there is *the entry into Jerusalem*, where Jesus redefines kingship. He comes like David—he is welcomed as the Son of David. Yet he doesn't come in as the warrior king; he doesn't storm the city. He comes in as the peace king riding on a donkey. Matthew quotes Zechariah: "Look, your king is coming to you, humble, and mounted on a donkey" (Matthew 21:5; Zechariah 9:9). In his book *Binding the Strong Man*, Ched Myers says that the so-called triumphal entry is "a misnomer" and is "carefully choreographed political street theater" designed to repudiate messianic triumphalism.[9] Jesus is rejecting the way of power, violence and the warrior, and instead is reflecting the Prince of Peace from Isaiah 9:7, whose

> authority shall grow continually,
>   and there shall be endless peace
> for the throne of David and his kingdom.
>   He will establish and uphold it
> with justice and with righteousness
>   from this time onward and forevermore.

The next day *Jesus turns the tables* in the temple—the next sign. The tables of exploitation are turned as Jesus quotes from Jeremiah 7:11. In this chapter Jeremiah is told by God to stand in the gate of the Lord's house and tell the people that unless they mend their ways there will be judgment on the temple. He goes on to say, "If you truly amend your ways and your doings, if you truly act justly one with another, if you do not oppress the alien, the orphan, and the widow, or shed innocent blood in this place, and if you do not go after other gods to your own hurt, then I will dwell with you in this place" (Jeremiah 7:5-7). He adds, "Has this house . . . become a den of robbers?" (v. 11). So, Jesus, like one of the prophets of the Hebrew Scriptures, is turning the tables of hypocrisy, of lives that don't match up. He's turning the tables of those who exploit, of those who use power wrongly, of those who manipulate and love money, of those who are greedy and yet claim to be worshipers. Jesus is saying worship encompasses all of life. It is a rejection of racial divisions, class, caste or religious superiority. It is a revolution of justice, love, wholeness and purity.

In *Jesus, Justice and the Reign of God* William Herzog points out,

If Jesus has assumed the role of a broker of God's forgiveness by reincorporating the outcasts into the people of God, he also believed that the temple was no longer necessary. His symbolic destruction of the temple, therefore, fits with the prophetic orientation of his public work. Jesus' rejection of the temple may well have derived from his analysis of the economic situation created by it. As the temple amassed wealth, the people of the land were getting poorer and poorer. . . . Jesus drew the logical conclusion that the temple was getting rich at the expense of the peasants, villagers and urban artisans. . . . Jesus made the temple a symbol of these economic forces by identifying it as the "cave of bandits." . . . Jesus' action in the temple then was an enacted parable or prophetic sign of God's judgment on it and therefore of its impending destruction.[10]

Herzog goes on:

Jesus did believe that the end of the old temple would lead to something new, but not a new temple. The destruction of the oppressive institution that the temple had become was one step towards the coming justice of the reign of

God, who gathers the outcasts and foreigners and invites them to build a community where, in the words of Isaiah "In righteousness [justice] you shall be established; you shall be far from oppression; for you shall not fear; and from terror, for it shall not come near you. Maintain justice, and do what is right; for soon my salvation will come and my deliverance shall be revealed."[11]

Herzog concludes, "The symbolic destruction of the temple was a prelude to the coming justice of a different kind of reign, the reign of God."[12]

The third sign of this holy week is *the washing of the disciples' feet*. As Jesus is doing this, it is the only time in the Gospels he refers to himself as "Lord." He says, "If I, your Lord and teacher, have washed your feet, you also ought to wash one another's feet" (John 13:14). And so Jesus is redefining the word *Lord* just as he redefined the word *King*. He is clearly modeling himself on the Isaiah servant, who has gentle spirit and who will bring forth justice to the nation. As Isaiah said,

He will not cry or lift up his voice,
  or make it heard in the street;
a bruised reed he will not break,
  and a dimly burning wick he will not quench;
  he will faithfully bring forth justice. (Isaiah 42:2-3)

This is the servant whose gentle spirit will lift people up. He won't crush or dominate people. Instead, he will allow justice to blossom. He is showing us that God's character is to serve.

Comparing Isaiah 42:1-9 with Isaiah 40:1-11, we discover that the suffering servant on whom Jesus modeled himself is one who will reveal justice—"the uneven ground shall become level, and the rough places a plain"—but also gentleness—"he will feed his flock like a shepherd; he will gather the lambs in his arms, and carry them in his bosom, and gently lead the mother sheep" (Isaiah 40:4, 11). And in both passages there is a sense of hope: "I have taken you by the hand and kept you; I have given you as a covenant to the people, a light to the nations, to open the eyes that are blind, to bring out the prisoners from the dungeon, from the prison those who sit in darkness" (Isaiah 42:6-7). Gentleness, justice and hope are at the heart of both the message and the lifestyle of Jesus.

The next sign is the institution of *the community meal*, which we call the Eucharist, Mass, Holy Communion or Lord's Supper. I have already talked about this being the meal that unites—or rather it should be. This is the moment when Jesus meets every need. It is the place where minds are changed, where prejudices are recognized and removed. As we take the bread and wine, it reminds us that God is inside us by God's own Spirit. It is the place to meet Jesus, the place to review our motives, the place where we find forgiveness, the place of starting afresh, the place where we draw strength for the task of linking arms with our brothers and sisters in the community. It is the place of relief and joy as we share in Jesus' death and resurrection. It is the gift of Jesus to equip us as servants, to follow the compassionate king and his upside-down kingdom.

Interestingly, the *Eucharist as protest* is a possibility. In Beit Jala, near Bethlehem, the huge separation wall being built by the Israelis is cutting off Cremisan Monastery from the people of Beit Jala, whom it has always served. So every Friday afternoon a Eucharist is held as protest at the route of this wall of separation. It is a significant piece of theater and protest. The meal of community, which should reflect the inclusiveness of the way of Jesus, is protesting the lack of relationships and community caused by the monstrous wall that separates. So this is a prophetic moment of kingdom versus empire. Everything looks as if the empire will win—it appears to have all the power. It brings separation and division, but the way of the alternative community brings down walls of division and works for community, justice and peace. It may not happen fast, but it is a prophetic reminder that the day of justice will come. When I, along with others, visited the Eucharist, they thanked us for "being Christ to them."

Amos Trust's operations manager, Nive Hall, also took a group to the Eucharist at Cremisan. He was leading a group who were rebuilding a demolished house. (Over 27,000 Palestinian homes have been destroyed by the Israelis since 1967, which causes terrible hardship for the families.) The rebuilding is both a protest and a sign of hope. Nive expresses passionately both the sense of protest and the healing that the Eucharist brings.

> *Jesus is walking through the valley.* The day began with wind and rain on the building site in Battir; it was impossible to even see the centre of the village at the bottom of the valley. We started to move some blocks but, after an hour, work was abandoned for the day.
>
> We decided to go to Al Walaja, site of our previous home rebuild, to visit the family in their rebuilt home and to see how much the separation wall had grown around the village. We would then go on to the protest mass, which happens each Friday afternoon, at Cremisan monastery, just outside Bethlehem.
>
> Al Walaja is bittersweet. My heart soars to meet the family, to drink coffee and share stories of friendships made, bridges built and hope nurtured. Tears flow from tales of lives changed.
>
> But this is the frontline. The wall and its offspring road are here and growing, the beautiful valley is being ripped in two.

And then there is the "tunnel house." A family has the "right" papers to prove they belong to this land but they [the Israeli army] put them on the "wrong side of the line." The "solution" is to literally wall them in to their own private prison at a cost of $1 million. It is obscene.

It is obscene that these people in this village are being brutally shown by the wall, the settlements, the demolition orders, the soldiers and the bottomless budget that *we want what is yours but we do not want you.* We will dehumanize and humiliate you and make simple things so difficult. We will make your life so intolerable that you will leave.

I am furious and helpless as we move on to Cremisan. Our voices and actions seem so small in the face of the inevitability of what we have seen. The battle has been lost.

How can the world stand by and let this happen? How can God?

The monastery at Cremisan is also facing the loss of much of its land to the wall and this weekly mass is part of their resistance.

We gather in an olive grove and the priest arrives and sets up a simple altar. We are welcomed and encouraged in English and then the mass begins.

A tangible feeling settles on us, a presence.

We share the peace and it is not a furtive handshake and a clichéd phrase. Instead, we open our hearts to each other.

We queue for the sacrament and feel welcomed to this table. The priest looks me in the eye and says "the body and blood of our Lord Jesus Christ" as he lays the wafer on my tongue. Never has this felt so real.

In this act Jesus is walking through this valley. He weeps with his children and enables them to stand, to remain, to speak and to act.

This is true communion.[13]

The most significant sign of all—the cross—is our example and our route. It is at the heart of our faith and is the route that Jesus now takes. I remember once when I was in Malaysia meeting with Archbishop Anthony Soter Fernandez, who was the Catholic archbishop of Malaysia. (He is now the archbishop emeritus of the Catholic Archdiocese of Kuala Lumpur.) When he was installed he chose two quotations—one by Dietrich Bonheoffer: "When the Lord calls, he bids us come and die," the second from Galatians 1:10: "If I were still pleasing people, I would not be a servant of Christ." The archbishop is a man of tremendous courage and deep understanding of the implications of the gospel. The security police came to his home on one occasion in the middle of the night. Echoing Jesus talking to the temple police, he said to the security men, "only robbers call at night." So he insisted they sign the guest book so that he could treat them as guests. It is quite amusing to look at his guest book and see the string of names. He knows that following the way of Christ needs to be a way of courage. Indeed, it could be a journey to crucifixion.

Jesus had challenged the domination system of his day in the name of God, and he was killed for it. He stood against the kingdoms of this world and introduced the kingdom or reign of God. And when we stand up against the domination systems of our day, we too may suffer. But Jesus has called us to take up our cross and follow him. This is why we campaign on issues, trying to name the power and stand against the domination system.

The cross can also be a sign of comfort, particularly to those who feel alienated. The Dalits see special symbolism in the cross. They say that Jesus' humanity and his divinity are to be understood in terms of his dalitness, or brokenness, and that his dalitness is best symbolized by the cross.

A. P. Nirmal says,

> On the cross he was the broken, the crushed, the split, the torn, the driven-asunder and a Dalit in the fullest possible sense of that term. 'My God, my God, why hast thou forsaken me?' he cries aloud from the cross. The Son of Man feels that he is God-forsaken; the feeling of being God forsaken is at the heart of our Dalit experiences and Dalit conscientiousness in India. It is the Dalitness of the divinity and humanity that the cross of Jesus symbolizes.
>
> Brokenness belongs to the very being of God. God is one with the broken people. God suffers when God's people suffer. God weeps when God's people weep. God laughs when God's people laugh. God dies when God's people die and God rises again in God's people's resurrection.[14]

A moving letter from Naim Ateek of the Sabeel Liberation Theology Group speaks of the Palestinians as another group of people who identify with the suffering of Christ, but Naim goes on to the resurrection.

> As the disciples thought about Jesus' death and experienced in some way his resurrection, they saw these events as the story of victory over evil. They saw that the principalities and powers had been defeated in the work of the cross. They saw Jesus' death and resurrection as the road to forgiveness and one-ness with God, and so for commu-

nities and for individuals we have been shown a way to forgiveness and reconciliation.[15]

So the way of the cross is the way of love; from the cross streams love, reconciliation, forgiveness and hope. Inspired by the spirit of Jesus, we are called to be a community who reflects the values of God's reign—seeing the poor, the vulnerable, the outcast and the weak through the eyes of Jesus; being the hands of Jesus by reaching out with healing, hope and compassion to bring a community of justice.

If the gospel is good news and liberation for Dalits and Palestinians, for the poor and oppressed, so too is it for all of us in our different needs. Jesus saves us from mundane, materialistic lives. Jesus saves us from greed and obsession with ourselves, and liberates us from our burdens and guilt. He lifts up our eyes to have vision, to care for the needy, to campaign for justice, to live with thanks in our heart for this beautiful world. And if we know through faith the presence of Jesus beside us, we in turn see there is more to life. There is mystery, spirituality and even resurrection.

GOD IS WAITING FOR YOU

Archbishop Desmond Tutu, in an article in the *Telegraph* one Easter Sunday, said,

> There will be peace on earth. The death and resurrection of Jesus Christ puts it beyond doubt: ultimately, goodness and laughter and peace and compassion and joyfulness and forgiveness will have the last word.
>
> Jesus says, "And when I am lifted up from the Earth I shall draw everyone to myself," as He hangs from His cross with out-flung arms, thrown out to clasp all, everyone and everything, in a cosmic embrace, so that all—everyone, everything—belongs."

Then in an extraordinary little section at the end he talks personally to Gyles Brandreth, the interviewer, who does not claim to have faith—and it is very moving. Brandreth then says:

A final explosion of laughter and the Archbishop pushes back his chair and says "Come, we will go outside and watch the sun falling on Table Mountain and smell the flowers together. God is good, man, and he is waiting for you."[16]

I love those words: "God is good and he is waiting for you." God is waiting for us, waiting for our response, waiting for us to journey together in the community of love—the way of Jesus and justice.

After the crucifixion and the resurrection the disciples are told that Jesus has gone ahead of them. He is waiting for them. He has gone on into Galilee. Wherever we are, it is our Galilee where we are called to be disciples, where we are called to keep walking, and where we will always find that Christ has gone before us—a peacemaker in a world that has no peace. A healer in a world that is broken. A savior in a world that needs to be saved from its selfishness, its pride, its violence and its greed. A liberator who walks with us toward our wholeness, our humanity and our dignity, and though we may at times walk through valleys of despair and through times of crucifixion, we are never without this resurrection hope. We are part of the community of hope, the community of love, the community of Jesus.

Conversion is turning from the values of our world to the values of Jesus—in so doing we meet the one who forgives the past and provides motivation for the future. Conversion is saying yes to Jesus, yes to the ways of Jesus, yes to the values of Jesus, yes to the community of Jesus. We follow Jesus in baptism, remembering he was baptized by a radical political figure. Baptism is a sign of membership in the community of God, which takes part in and draws strength from the community meal. Saying yes is saying no to our prejudices and the emphases that we have wrong. It is saying no to selfishness, to the love of money and to militarism. It is putting the way of Jesus first, and loving others as Jesus would. It is saying no to the commitment to what theologian Walter Wink calls "the myth of redemptive violence," the view that violence can solve problems, which is common both to politics and Hollywood films. As Walter Wink says,

> The belief that violence "saves" is so successful because it doesn't seem to be mythic in the least. Violence simply appears to be the nature of things. It's what works. It seems inevitable, the last and, often, the first resort in conflicts. If a god is what you turn to when all else fails, violence certainly functions as a god. What people overlook, then, is the religious character of violence. It demands from its devotees an absolute obedience-unto-death.
>
> This Myth of Redemptive Violence is the real myth of the modern world. It, and not Judaism or Christianity or Islam, is the dominant religion in our society today.[17]

A couple of years ago I was with Ernesto Cardinal in Nicaragua. Ernesto is one of the most significant poets in the world. He is a Catholic priest and was part of the Sandinista government in the 1980s. I asked him whether he liked the term *liberation theology*, and he said, "I prefer the term *theology of revolution*." We chatted about that, and I thought in particular that the theology of the Sermon on the Mount is revolutionary.

It reflects a gospel that genuinely brings good news; it shows us how to live "do unto others as you would have them do to you." Therefore, we are not passive people; we are those who act, reflecting the values of God's community to bring change, to bring hope, to bring justice, to be an active part of God's revolution of love, humility, compassion and the peace of Christ.

PRAYER—GOD OF THE WISE CHUCKLE

God of the wise chuckle
Give me wisdom . . . and humour
Like an Archbishop Tutu—
He has wise words we need to hear
Like, "If you are neutral in situations of injustice,
You have chosen the side of the oppressor."

So teach us to beware of the word "balance"—
It means keeping things as they are
Preserving the status quo—
Where there is imbalance
We need to restore equality and justice.
Righteous God, stir us up
To be those who are passionate for what is right
So we do not fall into the temptations of silence, neutrality
 and balance
That see people in their suffering . . .
And simply leave them there.

QUESTIONS FOR REFLECTION AND DISCUSSION

1. "He was not Jesus of Jerusalem, Jesus of Rome, Jesus of Washington, D.C., or Jesus of London." What's significant about this observation for you?

2. What does *inclusive* mean? What does *exclusive* mean? Are there ways that you or your worship community might be exclusive? What would make your community more inclusive?

3. Discuss the author's portrayal of salvation: "Jesus saves us from mundane, materialistic lives. Jesus saves us from greed and obsession with ourselves, and liberates us from our

burdens and guilt. He lifts up our eyes to have vision, to care for the needy, to campaign for justice, to live with thanks in our heart for this beautiful world." In what ways are these experiences of salvation?

4. The author concludes, "We are not passive people; we are those who act, reflecting the values of God's community to bring change, to bring hope, to bring justice, to be an active part of God's revolution of love, humility, compassion and the peace of Christ." How do you, or your worship community, need to act for this to be true?

5. How do you feel about Archbishop Tutu's words "If you are neutral in situations of injustice, you have chosen the side of the oppressor."[18] Are there any situations, about which you are neutral, where God's Spirit might be nudging you to some action?

4

TIME FOR ACTION
Let Justice Roll

We as Christians cannot but speak out against injustice,
it should be part of our identity. We are doing this to
honor God. We are doing this because it is right.

MUNTHER ISAAC,
Bethlehem Bible College

Back in the 1970s I wrote a song called "Let Justice Roll! (Amos Rides Again)," originally titled "The People of the West." I was following some of the comments of the prophet Amos as I wrote it and bringing in some of the issues of the seventies (for instance, line one refers to Martin Luther King Jr.).

LET JUSTICE ROLL

We've silenced our prophets, we've shot down our dreamers
Our lifeblood is money, we're exploiting the poor
Oh, the people of the West just love to invest
In the system that keeps the poor world poor

We have no compassion; our lifestyle is evil
Higher living standard is the God we adore
Oh, the people of the West just love to invest
In the system that keeps the poor world poor

Let justice roll on like a river
Truth like a never failing ever flowing stream
Then tears of rage will turn to laughter
And people become what they should be

We ignore the ways of justice—though we talk a lot about it
We victimize the stranger seeking refuge in our land
Oh, the people of the West just love to invest
In the system that keeps the poor world poor

Greed is our mother, silence is our father
Our epitaph is written in frustrated tears of rage
Oh, the people of the West just love to invest
In the system that keeps the poor world poor

Let justice roll on like a river
Truth like a never failing ever flowing stream
Then tears of rage will turn to laughter
And people become what they should be

To my surprise I recently found this song used in an album of worship songs an Australian church had recorded. Their adaptation made me realize its ongoing relevance and importance. Whether related to situations in our own societies or in a long-reaching struggle like that of Palestine-Israel, the song is a cry for humanity.

In chapter two I said Bethlehem theology makes the kingdom/ community of God visible and carries on the task of the Prince of Peace. This is reflected very clearly in a prophetic yet loving document that has come out of the heart of Bethlehem, showing it is still a theology to shake the world and bring hope.

I first encountered the Kairos Palestine document "A Moment of Truth" a couple of years ago when I took an Amos Trust group to South Africa. (We work there with a project called Umthombo, which works with street children in Durban.) One day we went up to the University of Kwa-Zulu Natal in Pietermaritzburg to a center called Ujaama. This is a very practical theological center, and I wanted to ask them what liberation theology means in the new South Africa. Their answers were fascinating. This group of young women and men told us about their praxis—their action— the way they behave as a result of the gospel.

One of the last speakers, Solomuzi Mabuza, knowing nothing about us as a group, began by saying, "This is a Kairos moment for Palestine, and we are committed to supporting them." Our group was stunned. We were not expecting this. It was exactly our viewpoint—we had been campaigning on this issue for years. It took a little longer for Solomuzi to realize he had been at a concert of mine in the Peace Centre, Manger Square, Bethlehem, a couple of years before!

After a terrible attack on Gaza called "Operation Cast Lead," which proceeded from December 2008 to January 2009, I kept thinking, *It is a Kairos moment.* (*Kairos* means a significant moment—a moment of opportunity not to be missed; a cross-roads.) It was a brutal massacre: 1,385 Palestinians killed and 5,300 injured, compared to 9 Israelis killed (plus 4 by friendly fire) and around 100 soldiers injured.[1] The injustice was such that I felt we could no longer stand on the sidelines, trying to be evenhanded. The mountains must be pulled down, the valleys must be lifted up. "Enough is enough of brutality," I said as I opened the demonstration in Hyde Park on January 10. I kept thinking, *This Kairos moment, this crossroads, this special moment in time, how can we reflect it?* I also kept thinking about the "Kairos Document" produced in the 1980s in South Africa and the importance of that document in getting the world to wake up to the evil of apartheid. As Solomuzi said, "Now is the Kairos moment for Palestine."

Solomuzi was the first one to tell me that a Kairos document was being prepared in Palestine, in Bethlehem, and he put us in touch with Rifat Kassis, the coordinator of Kairos Palestine. Since then we (Amos Trust and many other partners) have put together a campaign to make people aware of "Kairos Palestine: A Moment of Truth." Subsequently, we have responded with "Kairos Britain: Time for Action" (kairosbritain.org.uk). (Churches in the United States have also responded with "Kairos USA: A Word of Confession and Faith from Christians in the United States," kairosusa.org.)

"Time for Action" is rooted in the call of "A Moment of Truth," which was written in the Bethlehem area and is now endorsed by the Christian leaders of Palestine. The document is a call for the worldwide church to respond to a Christian "cry of hope when there is no hope." They are asking for the church in each country to respond. The Kairos call is asking for equality. It is asking that Palestinians be treated as equal human beings. It is asking that we stop being one-sided and start being evenhanded.

Kairos Palestine: A Moment of Truth

The Kairos Palestine document is remarkable and loving, but also prophetic and challenging. It begins, "We, a group of Christian Palestinians, after prayer, reflection and an exchange of opinion, cry out from within the suffering in our country, under Israeli occupation, with a cry of hope in the absence of all hope."[2]

To the question "Why now?" they point out that a dead end has been reached in the tragedy of the Palestinian people. So they are addressing their brothers and sisters, members of churches and other communities in the land, but also the international community, their Christian brothers and sisters around the world, asking them to recognize the reality on the ground, the reality of the suffering.

In the second section they say, "We believe in one God, a good and just God." They address the fact that certain theologians in the West have adopted a theology that infringes their rights, such that the good news of the gospel has become "a harbinger of death" for the Palestinians. They ask these theologians to deepen their reflection on the Word of God and to rectify their interpretations. So they declare that any use of the Bible to legitimize or support political opinions or positions of injustice imposed by one person on another, or by one people on another, transforms religion into human ideology and strips the Word of God from its holiness.

In this same section they declare that the Israeli occupation of Palestinian land is "a sin against God and humanity" because it deprives the Palestinians of their basic human rights bestowed by God. It distorts the image of God in the Israeli who has become an occupier, just as it distorts this image in the Palestinian living under occupation.

In section three the writers address hope and affirm that their hope remains strong because, as St. Paul says, "If God is for us, who is against us?" They affirm that hope is the capacity to see God in the midst of trouble. They see signs of hope in their land, pointing out that the parish communities are vibrant and that most of the young people are active apostles for justice and peace. They also see local centers of theology as signs of hope. They recognize that many are determined to overcome past resentments and are ready for reconciliation once justice has been restored. They articulate the mission of the church to be prophetic, to speak the Word of God courageously, to stand alongside the oppressed as Christ did. They point out that the mission of the church is to proclaim the kingdom of God, a kingdom of justice, peace and dignity. Finally, they proclaim the resurrection as their source of hope. "Just as Christ rose in victory over death and evil, so too we are able . . . to vanquish the evil of war. We will remain a witnessing, steadfast and active Church in the land of the Resurrection."

Section four of "Kairos Palestine" picks up Jesus' commandment of love: "Just as I have loved you, you also should love one another" (John 13:34). The writers speak of our responsibility to love our enemies. They are clear that love is seeing the face of God in every human being, but this does not mean accepting evil or aggression on their part. Love seeks to correct the evil and stop the aggression. So they see resistance as a right and a duty for the Christian and that Christ set an example to resist evil, but not to resist evil with evil, which we must imitate. We must resist evil with methods guided by the "logic of love," and so resistance must be peaceful. They recommend engaging in divestment and in an economic and commercial boycott of goods produced by the occupiers—a nonviolent response. Through love they seek to establish foundations for a new society, for both Palestinians and Israelis, and they comment that "our future and their future are one." "Either [there will be a] cycle of violence that destroys both of us or peace that will benefit both." They call on Israel to give up its injustice toward them and not to twist the truth about the reality of the occupation by pretending it is a battle against terrorism.

Section five addresses the Palestinians' brothers and sisters—all of us around the world—and particularly their Christian brothers and sisters. The writers ask to be brought back into the communion of love. The communion of love says to every believer, "If my brother is a prisoner I am a prisoner; if his home is destroyed, my home is destroyed; when my brother is killed, then I too am killed." They call us to repent of our silence in the face of their suffering.

To their Muslim sisters and brothers they speak a message of love and of living together, and a call to reject fanaticism and extremism. They inform the world that Muslims are not to be stereotyped as "the enemy" or caricatured as "terrorists," but to be lived with in peace and engaged with in dialogue.

Next they address Jews, saying, "though we have fought one another in the recent past and still struggle today, we are able to love and live together." They say human beings are not made for hatred. A culture of love is a culture of accepting the other.

In section six, "Our Word to the Churches of the World," the authors express gratitude for the solidarity they have experienced, but call on the churches not to offer a theological cover for the injustices they suffer. They ask the churches to "come and see," come and see what's going on. Be pilgrims.

The document condemns all forms of racism, religious or ethnic, including anti-Semitism and Islamophobia, and they call on us to do likewise. They also call on churches to say a word of truth regarding Israel's occupation of Palestinian land.

Section seven asks the international community to stop using double standards and reject the selective application of international law. And in section eight the writers appeal to the religious and spiritual leaders, Jewish and Muslim, "to rise above political positions that have failed so far and continue to lead us on a path of failure and suffering."

In section nine "Kairos Palestine" asks the Palestinian people and the Israelis "to see the face of God in each one of God's creatures and to overcome the barriers of fear or race." The authors appeal to both parties "to reach a common vision built on equality and sharing." They point out how central Jerusalem is to this vision, and suggest that this is "where they will meet in friendship and love in the presence of the One Unique God."

Finally, the authors of the document end with their commitment to hope and faith in God. They believe that God's goodness will finally triumph over the evil, hate and death that still persist in their land.

TIME FOR ACTION

On Pentecost 2012 I attended a conference on the initial British Christian response to "Kairos Palestine: A Moment of Truth." The result of this conference was "The Iona Call." This call was the precursor to "Time for Action," which is a good and informative document showing the historical context of the conflict and the shameful role of Britain. "Time for Action" addresses Jewish-Christian and Muslim-Christian relations, and the theology that is often used to legitimize occupation. It also delves into the history of the Oslo Accords; the division of the West Bank and the encroaching of Israeli settlements; the impact of discrimination, home demolitions and the lack of access to water; and also the Palestinians' lack of access to Jerusalem. It raises the issue of the blockade of Gaza and the disproportionately severe violence of Israel against Gaza. The problem of Palestinian citizens within Israel, who are looking for the day they can enjoy full rights and equality, is examined, and this document remembers more than five million Palestinian refugees worldwide waiting to return.

Finally, there is a call to action, echoing the Palestinian call to action: "Are you able to help us to get our freedom back?" And "Time for Action" endorses the Palestinian call to "come and see," and reminds us to take political action, to respond with boycott, divestment and sanctions as nonviolent tools for justice, peace and security. It ends with a final challenge about the misuse of the Bible and encourages us to pray.

The conclusion of this British document reminds us that responding to the Kairos Palestine document

> involves difficult decisions and tough choices. However, the choice is not support for Palestine against Israel or vice versa. Rather:

- It is a choice for justice, against oppression; for human and political rights, against dispossession.
- It is a choice for freedom, against an occupation that denies freedom.
- It is a choice for equal human dignity, against racism and discrimination.
- It is a choice *for* non-violent resistance, *against* the violence that perpetuates a cycle of hatred and recrimination.[3]

The report ends with the words "We can be silent no longer. It is time for prophetic faithfulness. It is time for action."

HUMANITY OR OPPRESSION?

This aspect of Bethlehem theology shown in the Kairos Palestine document gives us hope and expresses it very clearly. It asks, "What is the church doing?" Are we on the side of humanity or oppression? When we clothe ourselves with compassion and with love, we will do something about what dehumanizes, about people who are warehoused and treated as worthless.

A quote often attributed to Francis of Assisi is, "Preach the gospel at all times, and if necessary use words." The gospel lifestyle speaks loudest. The Kairos Palestine document says, "Love is seeing the face of God in every human being. Every person is my brother or my sister."[4] It is a call to reject racism, to bring liberation and to be nonviolent. This threatens no one because it affirms both Israeli and Palestinian.

So, as members of the community of love our witness should be, "Don't let religion or power or wealth oppress" (see James 2:1-17). We believe in the revolution that says, "Those not valued are valued, those who appear insignificant are significant, the poor and forgotten are to be shown justice and hope."

I sometimes visit a church building in Nazareth that formerly was a synagogue. It is on the site of an even older synagogue, and somewhere close is the place where Jesus read the words from Isaiah about bringing good news to the poor (Luke 4:18-19), now called the "Nazareth Mandate." Here the one born into poverty, and who was previously a refugee, is explaining his ministry in terms of setting free the oppressed and proclaiming good news for the poor. This makes clear the ministry and work of the kingdom/community of God where all are included.

THE UNCHOSEN

I was listening to Dr. Peniel Jesudasan Rufus, a Dalit preacher, at All Hallows on the Wall (the church in London where I was guild vicar for fifteen years), and he was discussing how Dalits interpret theology. He said, "You see, when we come to the exodus story, we don't identify with the children of Israel conquering, we identify with the Canaanites, the Hittites, the Amorites, the Perizites, the Hivites and the Jebusites." They identify with those whose land is stolen, those who are treated as the "unchosen."

I was fascinated to hear this. Exodus 3:7-8 begins with words of deliverance:

Then the LORD said, "I have observed the misery of my people who are in Egypt; I have heard their cry on account of their taskmasters. Indeed, I know their sufferings, and I have come down to deliver them from the Egyptians, and to bring them up out of that land to a good and broad land, a land flowing with milk and honey."

Beautiful words! But read on, and there is a problem: "to the country of the Canaanites, the Hittites, the Amorites, the Perizzites, the Hivites, and the Jebusites." This is a word of liberation for some, but not for others. So we must be careful to realize this liberation was at the expense of others, and this gives us ongoing problems.

The concept of "chosenness" creates a problem, and we have to journey to where we recognize that all are chosen or none are chosen, otherwise we make God cruel and biased. We cannot favor one group and oppress another—not if we are to be faithful to the Bible. I was talking with a Jewish friend, Diana Neslan, about what chosenness means for her, and she said, "It is a responsibility to show light, justice and caring for others." Expressed like this, being chosen is positive and healing, not a way that dominates. It is a way that brings hope.

In this chapter we've looked at changing the systemic injustice present in one situation—a deep wound that has existed for over sixty-five years—and a theology that comes from the heart of the suffering that speaks directly to it in a prophetic way. Sometimes in churches there is a fear of speaking up too directly on an issue like this because it is viewed as too political. But as Archbishop Desmond Tutu said, "When people say that the Bible and politics don't mix, I ask them which Bible they are reading." Furthermore, it is part of our mission as Christians to address systemic injustice and speak to it in a prophetic way as both Bethlehem

theology and the Nazareth Mandate would suggest. This responsibility is reflected well in "The Five Marks of Mission," a very
helpful synopsis of the mission of the community of God, a
summary of the church's role in living out the gospel.[5]

The Anglican Consultative Council developed these five
marks of mission to show churches a complete way to reflect the
gospel. The Five Marks of Mission are used by Anglican and
Episcopal churches, the Methodist Church, the United Re-
formed Church, as well as a few others.

FIVE MARKS OF MISSION

1. To proclaim the Good News of the Kingdom

2. To teach, baptize and nurture new believers

3. To respond to human need by loving service

4. To seek to transform unjust structures of society

5. To strive to safeguard the integrity of creation and to sustain
   and renew the life of the earth

Churches normally reflect the first two or three points in a
very straightforward way. But when we get to the last two, a
problem occurs. How should we seek to transform unjust structures of society? And how do we strive to safeguard the integrity
of creation and renew the life of the earth?

The fourth mark of mission often is hardest for churches to
tackle because it calls for prophetic action and witness against
systemic injustice. It can be uncomfortable, but being prophetic
is part of the life of the church. It is part of the way of Jesus, part
of the way of the Hebrew prophets. The church is called to speak
truth to power.

In the Amos Trust a key aspect of our ministry is to encourage
churches to make this fourth mark a part of their ministry so

they can speak up and campaign for issues that reflect the justice of God's community. Talk is not enough. We have tried to make this mark visible in action, particularly as a response to the call from the Palestinian Christian community. For instance, over twenty-seven thousand Palestinian homes have been demolished in the West Bank since 1967, so Amos Trust has taken groups of volunteers to rebuild homes as both a sign and a protest against injustice, and to signal to homeless people that they and their communities are not forgotten.

Even as I have been writing this I have heard news of an adjustment of the fourth mark. It has been changed to: "Challenge violence, injustice and oppression, and work for peace and reconciliation." This is a helpful expansion and explanation of the previous wording. In my experience, challenging injustice must come before peace and reconciliation can be a possibility. Some would like to start with peace and reconciliation, but the order is important. The prophetic challenge leads to the possibility of peacemaking.

Put Some Legs to Those Prayers

Naim Ateek, one of the writers of the Kairos Palestine document, says,

I believe that Kairos Palestine is helpful because it lays out the reality of the situation, and toward the end it begins to talk about more active resistance and mentions about the Boycott, Divestment and Sanctions (BDS). I think we need to encourage our Christian communities everywhere in the world to know ultimately they have to act. They cannot just sit back and be satisfied with only praying for us. They have to put some legs to those prayers and try to do something about it. I believe more and more people in the world are

aware, or are becoming aware of what is really happening
and of the intransigence of the Israeli government, so I
think we need people to sit together and discuss what nonviolent actions they can take if they don't like BDS (Boycott,
Divestment, Sanctions). But I don't think it is acceptable to
just sit back and do nothing, because I think it is our responsibility as Christians to do something about this evil
that we are up against here for many, many years—and
people are suffering, people are totally dehumanized and I
think it is our responsibility as Christians.[6]

There is a problem today with the balance of ministry in
churches. Churches talk about pastoral care and spirituality but
quite often find it difficult to embrace the prophetic ministry.
This is also a difficult area for church leaders, partly because they
come in for criticism if they speak up. But the church has a responsibility to the prophetic ministry, and leaving it out means
the church does not truly reflect the values of the kingdom of
God. To speak the truth and stand for justice is part of the challenge of ordination to word and sacrament. Indeed, baptism
brings all of us into this prophetic community. So, if the church
ignores justice, it has lost its cutting edge.

Today many people have lost faith in the church and its
leaders. I am shocked by the number of my Christian friends
who no longer go to church; they are simply tired of the lack of
prophetic witness. One friend was going to join a church in a
village close to where he lived. On his first visit, gay people were
criticized and later so too were Palestinians. He spoke to the
pastor afterward to say he couldn't be in a church that exhibited
this prejudice. I think this is true for many people. The church
always seems to be saying no. The community of inclusion has
become a club of exclusion. And so prophets are frowned on

because they rock the boat. Of course they always did, whether it was Amos or Micah, John the Baptist or Jesus. When the church is quiet on prophetic issues and exhibits prejudice, it signals its own irrelevance and people walk away.

Naim Ateek says the church needs "a new revolution, almost like what's happening in the Arab world."[7] He is talking about a spiritual revolution, perhaps a "Christian Spring" that is prepared to affirm the rights of all people and to allow the wonderful inclusive gospel to bring its healing and hope. When Jesus came preaching the kingdom of God, it was active, it was political, it was a judgment on the empire of Rome.

Ateek went on to give a very thoughtful challenge to the evangelical community, which he sees as very important.

> This whole question of Empire is what we are up against now. I think evangelicals need to be aware of this, that if they are truly evangelicals with all the meaning of that word, then they have to begin to realize how much Jesus was active in giving a message of nonviolent resistance during his day. Also to become advocates rather than just recipients of a quiet understanding of Jesus who was never really involved. I think that's the challenge to the evangelicals, and we need the evangelicals.

This is an important challenge to be activists in God's revolution of love, to have the courage of prophets like Amos or like Martin Luther King Jr. to challenge corruption and injustice, and to reflect the values of the God who loves justice. Amos was revolutionary. As Ateek says, "He could see God in a different way than the way that all the people around him were seeing—this is a God who cares about what people are doing everywhere. . . . The message of Amos continues to be as fresh today as it was then."[8]

So the words of the man from Tekoa, on the hills around

Bethlehem, live on. They challenge us all as he calls for a revolution of caring for all. It is time to put legs to our prayers and let justice roll.

Naim Ateek's encouragement to put legs to our prayers remind me of Rabbi Abraham Joshua Heschel, who marched with Martin Luther King Jr. for civil rights. Heschel said, "When I marched in Selma, my legs were praying." I like that.

Prayer—God of Life Teach Me to Listen

God of life teach me to listen—
To know your protest over exploitation
To feel your pain over the tearing of the fabric of life and
    community
As the poor get poorer and the rich get richer.
I have heard the poor speak of their misery—
Of feeling the pain in their flesh—of their hunger
Of not being able to get healthcare for their children
So they die of easily curable diseases.
I have stood with the young man whose wife died in
    childbirth

Because the proper care was not available.
God of life teach me to listen—
It is not enough to say "We didn't know"
Or to say "When did we see you hungry?"
You are the God who says "Do it to the least."
Never has our world known such wealth—such skills—
Such healthcare—such education
Yet . . . such inequalities.

Future generations will ask "Why were you silent?"
God of protest at exploitation and misuse of resources
Can we claim to be followers—if we do not listen—

If we do not raise our voices—if we do not protest.
Lord give us your compassionate heart
And take not your spirit of protest from us.
Lord help us to remember and take up the cross of caring
And take not your spirit of protest from us.[9]

QUESTIONS FOR REFLECTION AND DISCUSSION

1. In what ways do "The people of the West just love to invest / In the system that keeps the poor world poor"? Who does this apply to?

2. Discuss this definition of Christian witness: "So, as members of the community of love, our witness should be, 'Don't let religion or power or wealth oppress.' . . . We believe in the revolution that says, 'Those not valued are valued, those who appear insignificant are significant, the poor and forgotten are to be shown justice and hope.'"

3. How does the definition of choseness as "a responsibility to show light, justice and caring for others" differ from your understanding of what it means to be God's chosen people?

4. How should we as individuals and as worship communities "seek to transform unjust structures of society"?

5. "Never has our world known such wealth—such skills— / Such healthcare—such education / Yet . . . such inequalities." Why is this? What can we do about it?

5

MONEY, WAR AND EQUALITY
Tackling the Big Issues

*I wonder . . . if having financial services
and arms manufacturing at the core of
your country . . . corrupts you morally.*

ALEXEI SAYLE,
The Metro, April 9, 2013

ETERNAL ECHOES

Eternal echoes are calling me somewhere on the wind
They're hard to hear—sometimes I fear I won't hear them again
But they return and seem to say you've somewhere you belong
Oh eternal echoes are leading me with the silent voice of love

We are what we do with our silence
It is the drawing back of the bowstring on the bow
And silence is the place we meet face to face
And silence is restoring me—it is the still small voice
Preparing me for all that is to come

Eternal echoes . . .

You meet me by the water in the morning
Say the boat that I must row cannot carry gold
Nor weapons to maim or kill—they will destroy my soul

So I must leave it all behind for a much much better way
Preparing me for all that is to come

Eternal echoes are calling me somewhere on the wind
They're hard to hear—sometimes I fear I won't hear them again
But they return and seem to say you've somewhere you belong
Oh eternal echoes are leading me with the silent voice of love

I was sitting in First Baptist Church in Managua with the Reverend Dr. Gustavo Parajon. The congregation and choir started to sing a song that sounded great to me, but not understanding Spanish I didn't know what they were singing, so he translated part of the song, which was inspiring. I had not heard the song before and didn't know if it was available in English, but it said we must reject gold, wealth and a commitment to arms, that there is a better way to live. I was writing "Eternal Echoes" (a song inspired by John O'Donohue's book of the same name) at the time, and in the second verse I reflected some of the words Gustavo said to me:

You meet me by the water in the morning
Say the boat that I must row cannot carry gold
Nor weapons to maim or kill—they will destroy my soul
So I must leave it all behind for a much much better way
Preparing me for all that is to come.

These words came across as a challenge. They include the challenge of the Christian lifestyle with its rejection of the obsession for wealth, power and materialism, and of the obsession with violence and militarism. So "Eternal Echoes" attempts to say something about the Holy Spirit's call to live the Jesus way.

A still small voice throughout the Bible challenges us to draw strength from pausing and meditating and being part of this community of love, God's kingdom. But at the same time we are reminded not to let our soul be destroyed by trying to carry "the gold" or "the weapons that maim and kill." There is a better way, and this is where the power of the gospel becomes so relevant, because it is an alternative way to the power of empire and domination. It is always for the benefit of the wider community, always for the common good.

This is why certain political views, or views endorsing selfishness, which have been dominant in recent times, have to be challenged. The Sermon on the Mount—the teachings of Jesus—does not accept this rejection of the community and this commitment to selfishness.

During the last US presidential campaign a strange thing happened: Mitt Romney chose as his running mate Paul Ryan, who is a Catholic and was welcomed by many Christians. Yet he is committed to the thinking of Ayn Rand, whom commentator Andrew Sullivan in the *Sunday Times* describes as

> the atheist radical individualist whose books celebrate the strong and mock the weak. Rand's ultimate virtue was selfishness; her ultimate vice, charity of any kind. She despised Jesus and his teachings about the blessedness of the poor, the tragedy of the rich and the need for radical selflessness if we are to become our true selves. Ryan isn't just a reader of Rand; he is a disciple. He required all his employees to read her.[1]

Ayn Rand is dedicated to selfishness. She sees selfishness as the highest way of living. Rand has two key thoughts: (1) that selfishness is the highest of moral virtues, and (2) that "the masses, above all resentful of success, are parasites living off the hard work of capitalists far superior to them in every way."[2] This is why Rand appeals to people who want to support the 1 percent, who have the majority of the world's wealth—she is overtly and virulently against the teachings of Jesus Christ in the Sermon on the Mount. It would be interesting to ask certain Christians why they felt it was positive that Paul Ryan, so committed to Rand's way, was a running mate of Mitt Romney.

The shocking idea embraced by Rand encourages those who dominate to hold on to the wealth and exclude others. There needs to be a theological discussion at this point to sort out exactly what the Bible says in terms of how we live, how we treat our neighbors, what justice is and how we use our money.

In 1 Timothy 6:7-11 we read:

> We brought nothing into this world, and it is certain we can carry nothing out.
>
> And having food and raiment let us be therewith content.
>
> But they that will be rich fall into temptation and a snare, and into many foolish and hurtful lusts, which drown men in destruction and perdition.
>
> For the love of money is the root of all evil: which while some coveted after, they have erred from the faith, and pierced themselves through with many sorrows.
>
> But thou, O man of God, flee these things; and follow after righteousness, godliness, faith, love, patience, meekness. (KJV)

So if we translate *righteousness* as "justice," then we "follow after justice, godliness, faith, love, patience, meekness." This is our way to live—we have a lifestyle to follow.

Further on in 1 Timothy 6:17-19 we read:

> As for those who in the present age are rich, command them not to be haughty, or to set their hopes on the un-certainty of riches, but rather on God who richly pro-vides us with everything for our enjoyment. They are to do good, to be rich in good works, generous, and ready

to share, thus storing up for themselves the treasure of a good foundation for the future, so that they may take hold of the life that really is life.

Luke 6:20-25 says,

Then he looked up at his disciples and said:
"Blessed are you who are poor,
    for yours is the kingdom of God.
"Blessed are you who are hungry now,
    for you will be filled.
"Blessed are you who weep now,
    for you will laugh.

"Blessed are you when people hate you, and when they exclude you, revile you, and defame you on account of the Son of Man. Rejoice in that day and leap for joy, for surely your reward is great in heaven; for that is what their ancestors did to the prophets.

"But woe to you who are rich,
    for you have received your consolation.
"Woe to you who are full now,
    for you will be hungry.
"Woe to you who are laughing now,
    for you will mourn and weep."

The Bible uses extraordinarily strong words about money. "Woe to you who are rich," and "Blessed are you who are poor for yours is the kingdom of God." The Sermon on the Mount turns things upside down or indeed the right way up. This sermon does not encourage the 1 percent. The poor are on the side of the kingdom/community of God, but the kingdom also brings hope to the rich—it shows them a way of life that will be a blessing to them because it doesn't leave them rich but does give

them the satisfaction that comes to those who hunger and thirst
for justice.

Rabbi Heschel observes,

> The most urgent task is to destroy the myth that accumu-
> lation of wealth and the achievement of comfort are the
> chief vocation of humanity. How can adjustment to society
> be an inspiration to our youth if that society persists in
> squandering the material resources of the world on lux-
> uries in a world where more than a billion people go hungry
> every night? . . . [We must insist] that life involves not only
> the satisfaction of selfish needs, but also the satisfaction of
> a divine need for human justice and nobility.[3]

The love of money, the love of violence and the establishment
of inequality are three aspects endorsed by empire and stand
against the values of the way of Jesus and Bethlehem theology.
First Timothy 6:10—"the love of money is the root of all kinds of
evil"—is a direct challenge to the current structure of our world.

As I write this, the richest people in the world are meeting in
Davos, Switzerland. Of this meeting Aditya Chakrabortty says,
"More than 2,500 business executives and bankers will converge
on the highest town in Europe for the annual World Economic
Forum. For the next five days Davos will, it is safe to say, boast
more millionaires per square foot than anywhere else on the
planet." He points out there is a basic membership and entrance
price tag of £45,000 (approx. $74,000), but then adds,

> The real business lies in private sessions with industry
> peers and amenable politicians and access to those start at
> around £98,500 [$161,600].
>
> And this is what makes Davos so fascinating: it is the
> most perfect case study of how the practitioners of free

market, globalised capitalism give the public one explanation for what they are doing and why, while privately pursuing the complete opposite. On the one hand there is an event attended by Sharon Stone, Bono and a slew of tame academics (14 Nobel laureates this week alone) the message being, "we are open to anyone." On the other hand, there are those secret meetings off limits to anyone not in the £100k club. . . . From its inception, the whole point of Davos has been to promulgate the gospel of free market fundamentalism.

Earlier generations would have known what to call this Davos set of wealth extractors and rip-off merchants.[4]

Andrew Sayer, a lecturer from Lancaster University, is working on a book titled *Why We Can't Afford the Rich*. This brings to mind John Ruskin, a devout Christian of 150 years ago, who said, "There is no wealth but life." He argued for "people before profits." For Ruskin the positive use of money can be called "wealth," whereas money being used wrongly he calls "illth."[5] And today's hyperwealth by a few makes the community ill. As the superrich get richer, we find the welfare state disintegrates, community is torn apart, the planet itself is plundered.

Greed is not a way forward. We have to challenge the way of life where a few receive million-dollar bonuses (or several million) without blushing. For the sake of the gospel and the rich, we must proclaim, "Woe to the rich." We need to find a way to live in community, where we all share freely and value humility and simplicity. Then Bethlehem theology will become a reality.

When Luke presents John the Baptist's baptism of repentance for the forgiveness of sins (Luke 3:4-6), he quotes Isaiah 40:3-5: "every valley shall be filled, and every mountain and hill shall be made low, and the crooked shall be made straight." The way of

the Lord is justice and equality, and Jesus is baptized by this
highly political prophet, thus revealing the direction of his own
ministry. We encounter the same in Mary's song:

> He has brought down the powerful from their thrones,
>   and lifted up the lowly;
> he has filled the hungry with good things,
>   and sent the rich away empty. (Luke 1:52-53)

This is what justice looks like.

In an interview in *Third Way* magazine Baroness Helena
Kennedy says:

> I feel that what [Christian churches] really should be worry-
> ing about is materialism and the commodification of every-
> thing. What they should really be worrying about is the way
> in which we have made money a God. And there's plenty of
> churchgoing folks who don't want to challenge that.[6]

In explaining what *commodification* means, she talks about a
recent visit to the United States with her husband, who is a
surgeon. They found themselves sitting with surgeons who said
they wouldn't support any kind of healthcare system that would
cover the poor. She and her husband were puzzled by this—in a
rich country with so many Christians. The surgeons said they
didn't want universal health care because "they needed to max-
imize their income because they had had to pay a million dollars
to become so highly qualified." The baroness says this is what
happens to societies who commodify everything. "You are actually destroying the things that hold society together." She
would like to see churches being more vociferous on this.

At root, the love of money is idolatry: putting money before
God and the way of God. The result is the rejection of the
common good and community. Pope Francis has spoken out

clearly on this. In September 2013 he called for a global economic system that puts people at its heart and not "an idol called
money." Talking to an unemployed worker in Sardinia, he said,
"Where there is no work, there is no dignity." Then he added,
"This is not just a problem of Sardinia; it is not just a problem of
Italy or of some countries in Europe. It is the consequence of a
global choice, an economic system which leads to this tragedy;
an economic system which has at its centre an idol called money."
The pope went on to say that God wants men and women to be
at the heart of the world, "but now, in this ethics-less system,
there is an idol at the centre and the world has become the
idolater of this 'money-god.'"[7]

I used to live opposite a man who worked for a company
making arms, and he told me how successful their business was
and how much money they were making. One night protestors
came and put posters all around where he lived. The posters
showed people in the Iraq War who were bombed by the
weapons his company made. Later when we were chatting about
the posters he said, "They are right in what they are saying." In
other words, the wealth of his company depended on the brutal
destruction of people in Iraq. He was not an evil man; he was
not a brutal man. I think he was worried about what his company
was doing, but he accepted it as inevitable. If they didn't do it,
someone else would. The love of money can lead to the love of
war, not war in itself but the fact that the sale of armaments
makes people rich.

Countries such as Britain and the United States are committed to violence as a way to solve problems, even though
recent wars have failed miserably. Those of us who want to be
part of the community of love and to challenge empire need to
realize we cannot cross this line.

Philosopher, academic and activist Cornel West criticized

President Obama for putting his hand on Martin Luther King Jr.'s Bible at his second inauguration. West says,

> Why? Because Martin Luther King, Jr. died . . . for the three crimes against humanity that he was wrestling with. Jim Crow, traumatizing, terrorizing, stigmatizing Black people. Lynching, not just "segregation" as the press likes to talk about.
>
> Second: Carpet bombing in Vietnam killing innocent people, especially innocent children, those are war crimes that Martin Luther King, Jr. was willing to die for. And thirdly, was poverty of all colors, he said it is a crime against humanity for the richest nation in the world to have so many of its precious children of all colors living in poverty. . . .
>
> So I said to myself ain't nothing wrong with putting your hand on the bible, even though the bible's talking about justice, Jesus is talking about the least of these.

West continues,

> Brother Martin Luther King, Jr., what you say about the New Jim Crow? What would [you] say about the Prison Industrial Complex? What would you say about the invisibility of so many of our prisoners, so many of our incarcerated, especially when 62 percent of them are there for soft drugs and not one executive of a Wall Street bank [has] gone to jail. Not one. Martin doesn't like that. Not one wire-tapper, not one torturer under the Bush Administration—[at] all. . . .
>
> Then what would he say about the drones on the precious brothers and sisters in Pakistan, and Somalia, and Yemen. Those are war crimes, just like war crimes in Vietnam, Martin Luther King, Jr., what would you say?[8]

West is right. Martin Luther King Jr. took issue with war, violence and economic greed in society. King's prophetic and challenging voice on war and economic issues made him unpopular with many during the last years of his life.

After I sang at an event for Church of England mission agencies, some people wanted to challenge what I said about the Palestinian-Israeli situation. I was hesitant to do it, but I was persuaded to chat for five minutes. While one of the group was reasonable, two others were much more aggressive. At the end of our time, in an attempt to offer something positive that would link us together, I said, "Though you may disagree with us, let me assure you that whoever we work with is committed to nonviolence." One person responded, "Then you don't work with God." It took my breath away, and I think it shocked the more reasonable person of the group, who quickly brought the discussion to a close.

As I have reflected on what happened, I realize there is a certain logic in what the person said. A person can pick out a strand in the Bible to find a God of aggression, violence and even brutality. On the other hand we can also find another strand, a journey that leads through changes and developments in the Hebrew Scriptures to the nonviolent approach of Jesus.

Many people say, "Well, my view is the biblical view." Probably all of us would like to think ours is *the* biblical view. But then we end up disagreeing. There is a literal view that some people take that has only come about in the last couple of hundred years, and it can sometimes present God in such a way that we see a figure of bias and even cruelty. But I believe if we look at the teachings of Jesus and then follow them back to the Hebrew prophets, on whom Jesus based so much of his teaching, we discover a just and inclusive gospel that builds communities and rejects violence.

THE METHODOLOGY OF JESUS

Gustavo Parajon was a key peacemaker in Nicaragua, especially at the end of the Contra-Sandinista conflict. He and the Council of Protestant Churches of Nicaragua set up teams of peace commissioners working especially in the rural communities. Parajon said,

It is very important to think of the methodology of Jesus, which is the methodology of the suffering servant, and also of the poems that we see in Isaiah, and it can then be very clearly understood that violence is not redeeming in any way. Violence only engenders more violence, brings more violence. Jesus said the buck stops here, and he, in his suffering in his body, in his self, then absorbed violence and put a stop to it. And that was the redeeming factor because Jesus conquered over death. Even though violence thought it had won the battle by his death, yet because of his faithfulness he was resurrected on the third day. So this is very important for all of us to understand the methodology of Jesus; it is that of a suffering servant. And that is what makes a difference in the world, and it should make the difference in the Christian church in order to preach and share the good news that God loves all persons—men and women, white and black. God loves people and has then given us Jesus as a wonderful gift that has shown us that violence has no part in the plan that God has for the world.[9]

In an often quoted passage in Matthew Jesus says to his disciple trying to defend Jesus in the Garden, "Put your sword back into its place; for all who take the sword will perish by the sword" (Matthew 26:52). Peace activist John Dear says,

Matthew's version offers a reason for this commandment of nonviolence: "Those who live by the sword will die by the sword." Other translations put it this way: "Those who take up the sword will surely perish by the sword." With this teaching, Jesus addresses the world's downward cycle of violence and calls us to end it. Violence begets violence, Jesus says, so have nothing to do with violence. Break the cycle of violence with your creative nonviolence. If every Christian obeyed this teaching, violence would rapidly disappear.[10]

We struggle with this. As Christians we struggle with it, as we are embedded in societies involved in the downward spiral of violence. We are busy bombing societies thousands of miles from where we live; we are executing people without trial using drones; we amass stockpiles of nuclear weapons but threaten other countries if they even hint of building a nuclear weapon. That is extraordinary! We are sold out to the myth that violence solves problems. We forget that "those who live by the sword will die by the sword." We forget that we are told to beat our swords into ploughshares (Isaiah 2:4). We forget the wonderful old spiritual that reminds us to "study war no more," to "lay down our sword and shield, down by the riverside." We forget that Jesus told us to love our enemies. This is the hope of the kingdom/community of God.

There are, however, times when our communities seem to catch something of this message. I'll never forget the demonstration that tried to stop Tony Blair and his government from taking Britain into the Iraq War. It was a huge demonstration composed of a diverse group of people. It was a Holy Spirit moment. The country knew this war was wrong, and we were pleading with our leaders not to support it. As I write this, there has been another day of over a hundred people killed in Iraq. Thousands are dying there at the moment, the result of the Western invasion has caused so many deaths. The violence that was meant to solve the problem has multiplied it. Again recently when Prime Minister David Cameron asked Parliament to back the bombing of Syria in response to a chemical weapon attack on its own people, there was an instinctive reaction from the people, and Parliament rejected the request. This in turn prompted President Barak Obama to say he would take it before Congress, but before he could do so, President Vladimir Putin suggested an alternative, namely, for Syria to get rid of their chemical weapons. Clearly, people have had enough of war and are unsure that violence is the solution.

Luke 6:31 is a key verse that links all of this: "Do to others as you would have them do to you," which is mirrored in Matthew 7:12, "In everything do to others as you would have them do to you." In earlier times this was known as the Golden Rule. Rabbi Hillel, active just before and around the early days of Jesus, expressed this the other way around: "That which is hateful to you, do not do to your fellow. That is the whole Torah; the rest is the explanation; go and learn."[11]

How we treat others becomes crucial. If we are committed to the basic equality of all human beings as made in the image of God, then this not only affects the way we run our economy but also how we view weapons and their use. The fact that the church was pacifist until the time of Constantine is significant. The church then built a relationship with the empire, which of course led to the use of violence in support of the empire. Indeed the cross became a symbol of violence once Emperor Constantine had his famous vision in which God said, "In this sign conquer."

The Crusades reveal how Christianity was turned into a warlike religion. Christians first brutally attacked Jews en route to the Holy Land, then once there attacked Muslims. Because they did not realize Orthodox Christians lived in the land, they killed them too. It is a terrible story. My journeys in the Middle

East have made me realize how people still view Christianity as warlike, as they look back on the impact of the Crusades and then at current military invasions around the world that they see as Christian crusades—in other words, this is what Christians do. Indeed, President George W. Bush confirmed this by using the term *crusade* for the attack on Iraq.

Do we take seriously Jesus' attitude in the Sermon on the Mount? How do we view his warning that "those who live by the sword will die by the sword"? Is the use of drones moral when the kill ratio is 10 to 1? Even if we hypothetically accept that killing an alleged terrorist without a trial is justifiable, what about the ten others killed who are not alleged terrorists? Why do we "eliminate" people instead of arresting them? What is our justification? This does not abide by just war principles. And the way that President Obama has espoused the use of drones has caused his former supporter Cornel West to say that Obama "has now become head of the American killing machine and is proud of it."[12]

On September 22, 2013, as I was writing this book, over seventy-five Christians were killed at All Saints Church, Peshawar, Pakistan. Jandullah, the Taliban-linked group who claimed responsibility, said it was in retaliation for US drone strikes in Pakistan's tribal northwest. Violence does not happen in isolation; it affects communities. And those communities often respond in tragic and terrible ways. It starts with the brutality that hits their community, their families, their friends.

As Simon Jenkins said,

The greatest threat to world peace is not from nuclear weapons and their possible proliferation, it is from drones and their certain proliferation. . . . Drones are now sweeping the global arms market. There are some 10,000 said to be in service, of which a thousand are armed and mostly American. Some reports say they have killed more non-combatant civilians than died in 9/11.

I have not read one independent study of the current drone wars in Afghanistan, Pakistan and the Horn of Africa to suggest these weapons serve any strategic purpose. Their "success" is expressed solely in body count, the number of so-called "al-Qaeda linked commanders" killed. . . .

Neither the legality nor the ethics of drone attacks bear examination. . . .

It is hard to imagine a greater danger to world peace.[13]

WHERE THE WORST DICTATORS LIKE TO SHOP

Every couple of years an arms fair is held in East London, close to where I live. One happened recently. It is called DSEI (Defence and Security Equipment International) and describes itself as "The World's Leading Defense and Security Event." It is held in ExCel exhibition center. With the current situations in Syria and Egypt, there couldn't have been a worse time to host an arms fair. One headline said it all: "Where the Worst Dictators Love to Shop: World's Largest Arms Fair Comes to London."

Countries like Bahrain, Libya, Pakistan, Saudi Arabia and Uzbekistan, which have terrible human rights records, attend this event. So do countries at war like Afghanistan and Iraq.[14] Sarah Waldron from the Campaign Against the Arms Trade said, "This list reads like a roll call of authoritarian regimes and human rights abusers."[15] Groups of Christians, including London Catholic Worker, Christianity Uncut, Ekklesia and the Quakers, held services outside the arms trade fair to protest what was going on. There were other peace and justice activists, trade unionists and people from the Occupy movement. The Reverend Dr. Keith

Hebden and two other Anglican priests held an exorcism outside the arms fair. Hebden explained, "Just as Jesus called the disciples to cast mountains into the sea, by faith, we hope, by the same faith, to bring an end to terror with a price tag."[16]

It is very difficult to see Prime Minister David Cameron traveling with arms traders to different parts of the world, especially the Middle East, to exert as much power as possible to make arms trading successful. This will supply jobs in the short term, but what does it indicate for the longer term? What does it say to other communities around the world who see this? I'm particularly thinking about those involved in uprisings for human rights (for example, in Bahrain and the Arab Spring) who have these weapons used against them. The irony is that on his trip to encourage the sales of weapons, David Cameron laid a wreath at Amritsar, in the Punjab state of India, the scene of a terrible British massacre of unarmed people in the colonial days of the Raj. Which side of the struggle for freedom, justice and democracy is Britain on? The government's attitude toward the arms trade gives a clue.

Vijay Mehta has written a very challenging book: *The Economics of Killing: How the West Fuels War and Poverty in the Developing World.* He concludes the book with the following:

Across the world, the military-industrial system has willfully handed power to that 1 percent whose material desires can never be sated, who act as economic theory says they should—the leaders who murder, torture and steal in exchange for billions in a Swiss bank account, for a fourth yacht or a tenth palace. Such trappings are readily provided by Western corporations in exchange for unfettered access to the vast natural wealth of the developing world. Arms sales balance this trade and ensure that the avaricious kings and tyrants cannot be easily displaced, even by the violent insurgencies that pepper the poor world. . . .

However, millions are now realising that through collective action, unity and public awareness, this system can be torn down peacefully.[17]

Black Hawk Down

Inequality can affect the attitude of a whole society. It certainly affects the military's attitude. There is a very powerful film called *Black Hawk Down*, made by Ridley Scott (2001). In it an elite group of US soldiers drop into Somalia, and when one of their Black Hawk helicopters goes down, they find themselves in a desperate battle for survival. Nineteen American soldiers were killed in this raid. It is an extraordinarily intense war film. The most devastating moment of the film comes in the closing credits when we read the names of the nineteen American solders killed, and then we read that over a thousand Somalis were killed in this incident. Through the film we journey with the American soldiers, we empathize, and we are shocked that nineteen die, but up until the closing credits there is not a moment of sympathy for the thousand Somalis who died in the same incident. The imbalance is deeply shocking, and the impact of this and other incidents meant that the US foreign policy in Somalia was changed. Nevertheless, it reflects a common attitude among many nations, including the United States and Britain.

During the war on Iraq, US General Tommy Franks pointed out that enemy deaths were not counted. In striking terms he said, "We don't do body counts." Yet we count our own dead. This attitude indicates that we do not have an equal commitment to the people of other countries. We are there to change them so they are more in line with our system. Indeed, we may believe we are there to change the country for the better, but we still refuse to treat people as our equals. This problem is tied in with the arms trade and the use of violence to try to create better circumstances around the world. This of course implies that the rich and powerful countries are better, and their people are more valuable and significant. Indeed, the others should be grateful that we are bringing them our ways.

Equality Makes Us Happier—It Is Closer to God's Value of Justice

A very significant battle is taking place over the issue of equality. The 1 percent and their supporters fear that an alternative pattern of life will produce a socialist world, which they feel would be negative. Others call for equality because they believe each person is made in the image of God; therefore all are of equal value. Jesus' statement "do to others as you would have them do to you" ties in very well with this approach. Unless we take Jesus' words seriously, there will be no equality and therefore no justice. We cannot achieve justice through violence.

How we refer to others indicates our attitude. For instance, people sometimes use the term *lowlife* to describe a certain section of society. To even use that phrase is blasphemy. This term, and others like it, is not acceptable. Archbishop Desmond Tutu says, "Human beings are very important because they are 'God carriers' . . . they are tabernacles . . . carriers of the Holy Spirit. We should genuflect in front of each one like we do in front of the blessed sacrament."[18]

I heard the archbishop speak at Lancing College in Sussex, England, as he was dedicating a window to Archbishop Trevor Huddleston, who campaigned against apartheid. Tutu said Huddleston's God was "Notoriously biased in favor of the poor, the downtrodden, and those without clout." If we treat certain people as nonpersons because they belong to the wrong race, if we degrade them because they are powerless or we push them outside of the benefits of society, we fail to live up to the high value for humans reflected in the Bible. And because this is God's attitude to humans, we are in fact blaspheming.

A commitment to the poorer members of society runs throughout the Bible. And research has shown that equality makes us happier.[19] Inequality leads to the loss of community, which tears society apart. When we are very unequal we lose the sense of community. We lose our sense of mutual dependence. In one sense the isolation that comes to some wealthy people— isolation that has perhaps been longed for, the "gated community" mentality—makes them lose the benefit of the community and become more isolated.

A New Global Goal: End Extreme Wealth by 2025

A recent report from Oxfam is titled "The Cost of Inequality: How Wealth and Income Extremes Hurt Us All."[20] It starts off saying,

> The world must urgently set goals to tackle extreme inequality and extreme wealth. It is now widely accepted that rapidly growing extreme wealth and inequality are harmful to human progress, and that something needs to be done. Already we hear the World Economic Forum's Global Risk Report rated inequality as one of the top global risks of 2013. The IMF and the Economist agree. Around the world, the Occupy protest demonstrated the increasing public anger and feeling that inequality has gone too far.
>
> In the last decade, the focus has been exclusively on one half of the inequality equation—ending extreme poverty. Inequality and the extreme wealth that contributes to it were seen as either not relevant, or a prerequisite for the

growth that would also help the poorest, as the wealth created trickled down to the benefit of everyone.

There has been great progress in the fight against extreme poverty. . . . [But] we cannot end poverty unless we end inequality rapidly.

That is why we are calling for a new global goal, to **end extreme wealth by 2025** and reverse the rapid increase in inequality seen in the majority of countries in the last twenty years.

The following subheads provide a summary of the document:

- Extreme Wealth and Inequality Is Inefficient
- Extreme Wealth and Inequality Is Politically Corrosive
- Extreme Wealth and Inequality Is Socially Divisive
- Extreme Wealth and Inequality Is Environmentally Destructive
- Extreme Wealth and Inequality Is Unethical
- Extreme Wealth and Inequality Is Not Inevitable

This extraordinary call "to end extreme wealth by 2025" has the prophetic challenge of "woe to the rich" and an echo of Ruskin's words on "illth" and the need to rebalance our world. Back again to valleys being lifted up and mountains being brought low.

Churches could have a key part in this by showing that they are indeed communities of love of justice visible to the whole community. All churches could have the discussion, How do we do this? How do we live out the values of God shown so clearly in the birth of Jesus? God's revolution of love—a genuine revolution—takes courage, honesty and a return to biblical principles that are largely ignored. It will require humility, perhaps when kneeling to receive the Eucharist, where we come with our prejudices and bias, and leave them there. It might be painful. We might bring our weapons to church, as they did in Mozambique, and turn them into something beautiful for God (see chap. 6). Whatever we do, we will encounter "God with us." God has gone ahead of us and is calling us to follow, to be those who live out the good news and bring justice.

Prayer

God of the just heart
In the challenging words of the Sermon on the Mount—
"Blessed are those who hunger and thirst for justice
They shall be satisfied"—
You remind us that satisfaction does not lie where we
    might expect it—
In the security of wealth and privilege—
But in the joy of doing what is right
And in working to assert the value and dignity of other
    people
Because this is the calling of your community
This builds relationships and just societies
This brings deep satisfaction
As all are made welcome.

So keep us hungering and thirsting
For the values that make us all whole
And then we know the healing fountains will start.[21]

HUMANITY HANGING FROM A CROSS OF IRON

In a speech in 1953, US president Dwight D. Eisenhower said,

Every gun that is made, every warship launched, every rocket fired signifies, in the final sense, a theft from those who hunger and are not fed, those who are cold and are not clothed. The world in arms is not spending money alone. It is spending the sweat of its laborers, the genius of its scientists, the hopes of its children. . . . This is not a way of life at all, in any true sense. Under the cloud of threatening war, it is humanity hanging from a cross of iron.[22]

LITURGY OF EXORCISM AND REPENTANCE

A number of Christians, including three Church of England priests, carried out an exorcism to remove the evil of the arms trade. The liturgy, written by Chris Howson and Keith Hebden and used by kind permission, repents of our role in allowing the arms trade to continue.

LEADER   Let the earth bear witness

ALL   **Let the skies rejoice**

LEADER   We come as we are

ALL   **With faith, hope, and love**

LEADER   We gather together

ALL   **May our souls unite in the dignity of difference.**

Sisters and brothers, we gather to exorcise the demons of Militarism and Violence: To call an end to the evil horrors of the arms trade and to cast out the spirit of warfare and barbarism from this place. We remember Hiroshima and Nagasaki, the continuing global arms race, the failure of the nuclear powers to observe their obligations under the

Non-Proliferation Treaty, the polluted earth, the world governed by fear instead of justice, the futility of deterrence, the waste of public money, the horrors witnessed by Syria, Iraq, Rwanda, Palestine, Egypt, Democratic Republic of Congo. We call for peace instead of war!

The Peace of the earth be with you,
the peace of the heavens too;
the peace of the rivers be with you,
the peace of the oceans too.
Deep peace falling over you.
God's peace growing in you. (x2)

Almighty and ever-living God, you sent your only Son into the world to cast out the power of Satan, spirit of evil, to rescue humanity from the kingdom of darkness, and bring us into the splendor of your kingdom of light. We pray for all who attend this arms fair: set them free from the sins of greed and violence, make them instead a sign of peacemaking, a sign of resistance to militarism, make this place a temple of your glory, and send your Holy Spirit to dwell in this place. We ask this through Christ our Lord.

ALL   **Amen**

We cast out Satan and call for an end to the arms trade (**Amen!**)

An end to people's inhumanity to people (**Amen!**)

We cast out the spirits of greed and profiting from the suffering of others (**Amen!**)

We call on an end to the evil of cluster bombs, drones, rifles, instruments of torture—we cast you out in Jesus' name! **(Amen!)**

Holy water is cast onto the ground of the entrance to the arms fair.

Open prayers to remember the horrors of war and those involved in the preparation for war.

Sing (Taizé): Stay with me, remain here with me, Watch and pray, watch and pray.

LITURGY OF REPENTANCE

LEADER   We have come this day to worship God with a sign of our repentance.

VOICE   Christ has overcome the power of the shadow of death.

Yet still we tread in the valley of the shadow of death.

We do not always live as followers of Christ in the world.

We do not walk his way of justice, truth and peace.

So we repent.

ALL   **Father forgive us, we know not what we do.**

VOICE   We repent our government's involvement with
               the arms trade.

ALL   **Father forgive us, we know not what we do.**

VOICE   We repent our imagining such weapons could
               be aimed at our brothers and sisters.

ALL   **Father forgive us, we know not what we do.**

VOICE   We repent that we have not prevented this
               hidden violence.

ALL   **Father forgive us, we know not what we do.**

VOICE   We repent the hypocrisy of allowing the sale
               of weapons while condemning their use on
               civilians.

ALL   **Father forgive us, we know not what we do.**

VOICE   We repent of all those lives that we put at risk
               by our folly.

ALL   **Father forgive us, we know not what we do.**

VOICE   We repent the squandering of the people's
               taxes.

ALL   **Father forgive us, we know not what we do.**

VOICE   We come to this place

               as a sign of our willingness to change our ways,

               to name that which is sin.

We come to this place

as a witness to our will to change, to stand firm,

and to resist evil and it's embodiment in the arms trade.

ALL **Father forgive us, we know not what we do.**

LEADER Lord, you are merciful to all and hate nothing you have created. You forgive the sins of humankind and bring us to repentance. Protect us in our struggle against evil. Make this day a holy celebration of your goodness to us and bless our efforts to do your will. Amen.

Blessing One Another with Peace

LEADER Peace is not the product of terror or fear.

Peace is not the silence of cemeteries.

Peace is not the silent result of violent repression.

Peace is the generous, tranquil contribution of all to the good of all.

Peace is dynamism. Peace is generosity.

It is right and it is duty.

VOICE The peace of God be always with you!

ALL **And also with you.**

We share with one another a sign of the peace of Christ.

Let us go forth in peace,

In the name of Christ, Amen.[23]

QUESTIONS FOR REFLECTION AND DISCUSSION

1. Is there a danger that we "celebrate the strong and mock the weak"? How might we do that in our own lives or communities?

2. What are the indications that "the accumulation of wealth and the achievement of comfort are the chief vocation of humanity"? How close to home do we see this evidenced?

3. Discuss Gustavo Parajon's statement that "violence is not redeeming in any way. Violence only engenders more violence." Or as John Dear interprets Jesus' words: "Jesus addresses the world's downward cycle of violence and calls us to end it. Violence begets violence, Jesus says, so have nothing to do with violence." How do you understand this in relation to the Old and New Testaments?

4. How did you feel to read, "The church was pacifist until the time of Constantine. . . . The church then built a relationship with the empire, which of course led to the use of violence in support of the empire"?

5. How do you feel about the author's discovery that people of the Middle East "still view Christianity as warlike, as they look back on the impact of the Crusades and then at current military invasions around the world that they see as Christian crusades—in other words, this is what Christians do"? How do you think Middle Eastern people might reasonably respond?

6. How do you understand Baroness Kennedy's statement, "That's what happens to societies when you commodify everything, whether it's education or whatever"?

7. The author says, "God's revolution of love—a genuine revolution—takes courage, honesty and a return to biblical principles that are largely ignored." What topics or issues does your community need to be honest and courageous about?

GOD'S REVOLUTION OF LOVE

> *If you are neutral in situations of injustice,*
> *you have chosen the side of the oppressor.*
>
> ARCHBISHOP DESMOND TUTU

GOD'S REVOLUTION OF LOVE

We're trying to live by God's revolution—
God's revolution of love
We're trying to live by God's revolution—
God's revolution of love

By doing to others what we would want—
What we would want done to ourselves—
By loving our neighbours—loving our enemies
God's revolution of love

The rich and the poor will share with each other
In God's revolution of love
We'll tear down the walls that keep us apart
In God's revolution of love

By beating our swords into the ploughshares
That build community life
We'll stop making arms—that maim and destroy
In God's revolution of love

Jesus is with us—Jesus the worker
In God's revolution of love
Jesus the human—the teacher will lead us
In God's revolution of love

We're trying to live by God's revolution—
God's revolution of love
We're trying to live by God's revolution—
God's revolution of love

"God's Revolution of Love" is a vision of what God's revolution should look like. The song is a reminder of how we should be living—loving neighbors, loving enemies, sharing with one another—so walls of separation come down, so society is more equal, always following the example of Jesus.

I wrote the song a few years ago after going to church in Mozambique. It was a little Salvation Army church, basically a hut made of reeds. Their only instrument was a drum; they sang to us, and I sang to them. It was a very moving encounter. I recognized how far the country had come, because twenty years earlier I had been there with my son Tom during a time of civil war. We heard the sounds of war, particularly at night, and couldn't travel far outside Maputo, the capital city. We were hosted by Bishop Dinis Singulane, the bishop of Lebombo, a remarkable man with a passionate commitment to peace and nonviolence. He showed us something of God's revolution of love in action. He called on people to bring their guns, even children's toy guns, to church, where they were broken down and made into sculpture. So something creative and beautiful was made out of symbols of death and violence.

Being back in Mozambique and seeing the results of a revolution that brought a new way for Mozambique, this now peaceful country, was an important lesson. So, to remind us that this revolution of love brings us all together, I wrote a song that could be sung both in a little church made of reeds and in a grand cathedral.

When we were in Mozambique twenty years ago, Bishop Dinis showed Tom children lying on the street close to where he lived. The bishop was keeping an eye on them and helping them. I had no idea what effect this had had on my son. I didn't realize that it would completely change his life, which he has dedicated to working with street children and campaigning on their behalf. Now I was back there with my son Tom and his wife, Bulelwa (Mandi), who was a former street child herself. They had invited my wife, Gill, and me to visit. I couldn't believe what a different country Mozambique had become. This beautiful place, not without its problems, had come such a distance from its time of the civil war. It was a reminder that prophetic churches can help bring healing, hope and justice to communities where justice is currently hidden.

THE SPIRITUAL JOURNEY

I hope this book encourages us on our spiritual journey and toward being activists. It is very powerful when these two go together. On our journey so far, Bethlehem theology has pointed us to a way of life, the way of the kingdom/community of God. This way is humble, simple. It's the way of justice, the way where we get the right perspective on money, where we are not controlled by the myth of redemptive violence, where we value all human beings equally.

"God with us" identifies with those who are ignored or forgotten. This was prophesied in the Magnificat, the song of Mary, one of the most remarkable passages of the Bible. After Mary is told by the angel that she will have a son who is to be named

Jesus, she is also told that her relative Elizabeth is expecting a baby—the future John the Baptist. So Mary sets out to visit Elizabeth. When they exchange greetings, Mary breaks into a song that clearly portrays God's revolution of love:

> He has shown strength with his arm;
>> he has scattered the proud in the thoughts of their
>>> hearts.
> He has brought down the powerful from their thrones,
>> and lifted up the lowly;
> He has filled the hungry with good things,
>> and sent the rich away empty. (Luke 1:51-53)

This is the revolution.

The Magnificat is not so different from what we have already heard in Isaiah 40:4 about valleys being lifted up and mountains being made low. This is a vision of God's revolution of love, straightening things out so justice becomes visible in the community. The just God is also a gentle God, as we see in Isaiah 40:11: "He will feed his flock like a shepherd; he will gather the lambs in his arms, and carry them in his bosom, and gently lead the mother sheep." So this is both a just and a gentle revolution. As the baby is born in Bethlehem every aspect of his birth and life and death spell out this vision of hope, this vision of equality—that God loves justice. And how does God carry on this work today? We are called to be the hands of Jesus, to be the feet of Jesus, to allow the heart of Jesus to guide us and inspire us. Living this way makes visible the kingdom of God, the way of God, and the lifestyle of the community of God.

BE THE HANDS OF JESUS

Be the hands of Jesus
Be the feet of Jesus
Let the heart of Jesus be our guide

I was hungry you gave me food
I was thirsty you gave me drink
I was a stranger and you welcomed me
I was naked and you clothed me
I was sick or in prison and you came

Be the hands . . .

I was treated as an outcast
I was forgotten—I was despised,
But you helped restore my dignity
You gave me back my will to live
Because of you I rise in hope again.

Be the hands of Jesus
Be the feet of Jesus
Let the heart of Jesus be our guide

Everything is coming together at this point—we see this long-promised revolution becoming a reality, but it has to be lived out in community. Some Christians have interpreted their faith in a strictly personal way and do not understand that this revolution should make a difference in how we live in the community and how we bring justice to the world.

In the past we demanded that people assent to right teaching; sometimes people were even killed because they didn't. But now we recognize that God is made visible in right actions, in the way we live as community, as members of God's kingdom. We find

our value in our relationships with others. It is what Archbishop
Tutu calls, "a tender network of interdependence." These are
beautiful and important words and reflect his understanding of
the African word *Ubuntu*:

> We say a person is a person through other persons. We
> don't come fully formed into the world. We learn how to
> think, how to walk, how to speak, how to behave, indeed
> how to be human from other human beings. We need
> other human beings in order to be human. We are made
> for togetherness, we are made for family, for fellowship, to
> exist in a tender network of interdependence. That is why
> apartheid and all those systems are so fundamentally evil,
> for they declare that we are made for separation, for enmity,
> for alienation, and for apartness. Ubuntu enables recon-
> ciliation and forgiveness especially when hearts have been
> inflicted with such pain. . . . This is how you have Ubuntu—
> you care, you are hospitable, you are gentle, you are com-
> passionate and concerned. Go forth, . . . conscious that
> everybody is to be revered, reverenced as created in God's
> image. . . . Go forth to demonstrate your Ubuntu. . . . Go
> forth to make the world a better place where you can make
> a difference.[1]

This "tender network of interdependence" is the way of Jesus—
the way of God's community. Archbishop Tutu clearly depicts
the evil of divisions. And society is unhappier as divisions widen.
Separation, apartness and enmity, the divisions caused by wealth
and greed, are the way of empire.

NONVIOLENT SUFFERING SERVANT

In Matthew 4:8-9 we find the third temptation of Jesus in the
wilderness:

The devil took him to a very high mountain and showed him all the kingdoms of the world and their splendor; and he said to him, "all these I will give you, if you will fall down and worship me." Jesus said to him, "Away with you, Satan! For it is written,

'Worship the Lord your God,
  and serve only him.'"

This was the moment when the temptations reached their climax. As Naim Ateek says,

The tempter was enticing Jesus to walk the way of empire. Is it possible that the essence of the temptation lies in the then-popular messianic tradition in which God's Messiah would come to establish his kingdom and crush his enemies? This tradition is embodied in Psalm 2:7-9, "You are my son; today I have begotten you. Ask of me and I will make the nations your heritage, the ends of the earth your possession. You shall break them with a rod of iron and dash them in pieces like a potter's vessel." The psalmist is talking about empire.[2]

In rejecting the temptation Jesus is not only rejecting the way of empire, he is redefining the tradition of God's Messiah. As Naim Ateek says, "He rejected the Son of David strand of the tradition and embraced the unpopular and enigmatic strand of the suffering servant, the suffering Messiah, the way of non-violence and faithfulness to God."[3] He rejected the warrior tradition for that of the Suffering Servant.

So Jesus' rejection of the way of empire is also a rejection of war and violence, domination and oppression. Jesus is also undermining the violence tradition in the Hebrew Scriptures. This has a huge implication for Christians. If the kingdom/

community/revolution of God that Jesus brought is directly rejecting the way of violence, instead showing God's justice, compassion and love, then we too have to do the same. This is the quiet revolution of gentleness, justice and hope.

From earliest times God's community of love has witnessed to nonviolence: "those who live by the sword will die by the sword"; "do unto others as you would have them do to you." This respect for others is deep in the heart of Jesus' teachings.

The Christian community must have a bias toward peacemaking. We need to listen to the pacifist voices within our community. I am not a total pacifist myself. I once heard Archbishop Tutu describe himself as not a pacifist but a peacemaker. I would echo that. I admire pacifists and feel that we need to hear their voices because we hear so much from the dominant powers of violence.

If it was not so sad it would be amusing that when people stand up for their own human rights, independence or freedom, we insist that they be nonviolent. Of course, I think this is the better way, but the strange thing is this demand comes from countries dedicated to violence. We have one rule for the powerful and another for the weak. But God's nonviolent revolution creates a community of hope.

SUCH A DANGEROUS, HOPEFUL DREAM FROM GOD

If we endorse the use of violence to solve problems, then we are not encouraging our societies to be just. One of the great revelations of the New Testament is that God does not seek a "day of vengeance" but points to another way through the example of the Prince of Peace. God does not stand with the 1 percent or people of status or domination, but identifies with the humble, the oppressed and those who are forgotten in our communities. We are told to "strive first for the kingdom of God and God's justice." If we fail to see that this means building a community of equality and peace and hope for all, we have a different gospel. Jesus came with this very political message about a new alternative community—the kingdom of God. This is the message of hope. The gospel is good news for all, not just for a rich or powerful elite. This is why Christianity is such a dangerous, hopeful dream from God.

The kingdom/community of God rejects selfishness and endorses all that makes for the common good, all that makes for a society of equality, Ubuntu, gentleness and justice.

EMPIRE LOSES ITS POWER

Dr. Mitri Raheb, pastor of the Evangelical Lutheran Christmas Church in Bethlehem, preached at a conference in Bethlehem in 2011 on the words "Blessed are the meek, for they will inherit the earth" (Matthew 5:5). He pointed out that it should read "Blessed are the meek, for they will inherit the land." He believes it was mistranslated, and that Jesus was originally quoting from Psalm 37, which is not referring to lands near and far, but rather to "this land, [that is,] the Holy Land." Jesus is saying, "the meek will inherit this land." Raheb continues,

> The Holy Land has had a long history with empires. The first empire to occupy our country was that of the Assyrians who stayed over 200 years. After them came the Babylonians; they were pushed out by the Persians. They didn't stay long because they were pushed out by the Greeks, who were pushed out by the Romans. Then came the Arabs, then the Crusaders, then the Ottomans, and then the British. Last but not least is Israel.

Then he adds,

> Think about it—which of these empires lasted forever? None of them, for they came and stayed for fifty, a hundred, two

hundred, four hundred years, and then they were all gone
with the wind. When you stand in front of empire you
cannot believe that it will ever end. Often I think our problem
is that we really think that empire is here to last forever. But
actually Jesus wanted to tell us that empire will not last.[4]

So empires come and go. Who remains in the land? "The poor
remain. Even now the people of the land who are successful emi-
grate, become part of empire. Those who are well educated go to
seek jobs created by empire. Who remains in this country? The
meek remain. Empires come and go, the meek inherit the land." He
says, "All empires will be gone because this land will be inherited
only by the meek. What [Jesus] actually wants to do through that
one verse is to release us from the power of empire. The moment
Jesus spoke those words empire lost its power over us."[5]

THE STILLNESS THAT RESTORES

It is good to be rooted in a spirituality that gives us the resources
to be an activist and to work with others to raise our voice for
justice. I find it helpful at times to pause and be quiet, to draw
strength in the stillness that restores. In chapter one we thought
about "God with sleeves rolled up"—the God of action who is
also God of the pause, God who restores our hope, God in the
beauty of nature who lifts our spirits. So we need the time to be
still to be renewed.

IN THE QUIET

In the quiet I come to you
I find strength to start anew
Breathing out and breathing in
In the quiet I come to you

I find stillness in the storm
Despite the struggles all around
What's done is done—take time to pause
In the stillness I come home

In the dawn I come to you
Past the piper's haunting tune
Morning creeping from the east
In the dawn I come to you

You raise my head—you lift my heart
Everyday—another start
You meet us in the simple things
In the quiet where we begin

Evening time I come to you
As the busy day is through
In the warmth of evening light
I bow my head—I come to you

You raise my head—you lift my heart
Everyday—another start
You meet us in the simple things
In the quiet where we begin

I am fortunate to live in an area of London where there are many beautiful churches—some very busy but others quite quiet. When I need to pray or simply be quiet over some special issue, I cross the river to Southwark Cathedral and pop into the chapel set aside for prayer. It has become a very meaningful place for me. All of us need a sacred space where we can go to be quiet or pray. It doesn't have to be a church; it could be a beautiful place in the country or by the sea, a place where we take stock in the stillness.

It's easy for activists to burn out. So I have done quiet days for activists. I use them as times to pause and draw strength, to get rid of the rush of life for a moment. In the quiet, things are put into perspective. Then we look at outstanding issues. We think about how we journey on in our campaigning.

I have friends who are struggling with or even leaving the church. Though they remain Christians, they can't accept the negativity of certain churches. They see and hear bad news instead of good news. I feel we need the community of a church, but it is helpful if it is a church that reflects the breadth of the "Five Marks of Mission" (see chap. 4). This book has focused on the fourth mark: "To transform the unjust structures of society," but what about the fifth mark: "To strive to safeguard the integrity of creation and sustain and renew the earth"? This too is a huge issue that needs our spirituality, understanding and action.

If your church has a justice and peace group, join it. Maybe it is an area group, that is, a diocesan group or one put together by various denominations working together. Join the group and find allies. A friend was in a church that had no group addressing justice issues, so with the permission of the vicar he started one. Our churches need to beware a selfish spirituality. Remember Martin Luther King Jr.'s sermon at St. Paul's Cathedral? It reminded us of a balanced and complete life that has things in the right perspective, loving God, loving our neighbor and loving ourselves.

Our corporate worship should reflect this too. It should not simply be about "me and God" but should reflect loving our neighbors and even our enemies. Worship needs liturgies, songs and prayers that reflect the balance of God's revolution of love and the freedom that comes with a simple way of life.

> *Jesus came to set us free from selfishness and human greed*
> *And Jesus came a humble birth to show us it's a joy to serve*
> *And Jesus lives beside the poor and he calls out "follow me"*
> *And his outstretched arms they offer me the freedom of*
> *   simplicity*

These lyrics are from the Christmas song "Don't Blame God for Christmas," which I wrote with Peter Meadows. The song is about some of the stresses of Christmas, and these words come at the end to offer an alternative way of hope. The song is prompted by these words from Matthew's Gospel: "Do not store up for yourselves treasures on earth, where moth and rust consume and where thieves break in and steal; but store up for yourselves treasures in heaven, where neither moth nor rust consumes and where thieves do not break in and steal" (Matthew 6:19-20).

Peter and Mary West reflect on the meaning of this teaching.

> A thorough reading of the Gospels shows that for [Jesus], the "Reign" (Kingdom) of God is not something apart from this world—it is the life of heaven breaking into human history to challenge the powers of evil that corrupt human life, and to mend what has gone wrong. To "store up for yourselves treasures in heaven" . . . and to be "rich towards God" . . . is to put your faith and hope in that Reign of God's justice, and the lasting transformation of life it promises. . . .
>
> True security comes from God's justice, which exposes society's failings and points the way to a new world. The response of Jesus' disciples must be to build together a new community of love and sharing, putting the justice of God into practice in the face of the world's corruption and violence.[6]

If we are seeking first the community of God and God's justice, then we will journey this route: a life of simplicity, loving our neighbors as ourselves and allowing Jesus' justice to be visible.

A SIMPLE LIFESTYLE

In the 1970s there was a series of books calling Christians to a simple lifestyle. One that had perhaps the biggest impact was Ronald Sider's *Rich Christians in an Age of Hunger*. In his epilogue Sider says,

> All we need to do is truly obey the One we rightly worship. But to obey will mean to follow. And he lives among the poor and oppressed, seeking justice for those in agony. In our time, following in his steps will mean simple personal lifestyles. It will mean transformed churches with a corporate lifestyle consistent with worship of the God of the poor. It will mean costly commitment to structural change in secular society.

He goes on to say, "Sadly I must confess my fear that the majority of affluent 'Christians' of all theological labels have bowed the knee to Mammon."[7]

Once again there are movements calling for simpler living. There are "transition towns" raising awareness of sustainable living. They're asking people to check the distance their food has traveled to their local market and to consider living in a more self-sufficient way within their neighborhood.

In *Small Is Beautiful: The Study of Economics as If People Mattered* E. F. Schumacher makes the point that the "current pursuit of profit and progress which promotes giant organizations and increased specialization has in fact resulted in gross economic inefficiency, environment pollution and inhumane working conditions."[8] Capital, he argues, should serve people instead of enslaving them.

A simpler life brings the freedom that many are looking for. We need to leave our planet in a suitable state for the next generation, and we need to link with others to find ways to encourage this to happen. Together, in community, we need to promote a simpler lifestyle to benefit the common good of all. We need to embrace a spirit of generosity and an awareness of others. This has implications for how we live, how we give, how we view other parts of the world and how we view our own society in relation to less-fortunate societies.

In a *Third Way* interview Helena Kennedy was asked, "How do you think Christians should be living?" She said,

> Simpler lives. . . .
>
> We have allowed the gap between rich and poor to grow, and I think we should be in some way trying to narrow it again. I do think you pay a price for creating huge inequalities in society. In fairness to the churches they have often taken a lead on this (and when they do, when they speak out about "faith in the cities" or about social justice, they are excoriated for it).[9]

The first time Michael Moore came to Britain I went to see him speak, and at the end he almost gave an altar call, saying, "You know in Britain you are worse than we are in the States, you even have such things as loyalty cards to places where you shop." He asked how many had a card and perhaps three-fourths of the audience put up their hands. He then encouraged people to come forward, and he cut the loyalty cards in half with a huge pair of scissors. As he did he said, "You are free!" and everyone cheered and clapped. It was a public demonstration against the idea of allegiance to a corporation. His message was: Don't be fooled into trusting corporations.[10] Simplicity sets us free from schemes that bind us. Simplicity looks out for others and also for our planet.

As Archbishop Tutu says,

The Bible sees us living harmoniously with God, with our fellow human beings, and with the rest of God's creation—and so, we must all be "green." We must be concerned about the environment, about pollution, about finding alternative sources of energy, about depleting irreplaceable resources, about the so called "hot house effect," about damage to the ozone layer, about deforestation, about soil erosion, and the encroachment of the desert—for God has sent us in his world to be stewards of his bounty. We are meant to rule over God's world as God would rule—gently, compassionately, graciously, caringly. We are meant to leave the world a safer and better place than we found it.[11]

So the revolution of love affects every aspect of life. Barriers that separate us need to be rejected. Christians live out the tender network of interdependence, and the kingdom/community of God makes visible a world of beauty, caring, sharing, equality and inclusion.

Occasionally, certain theological views evidence a lack of love for God's world. Because they assume some catastrophe must come in order for Jesus to return, they look for and are encouraged by a downhill slope of destruction. This fails to understand that we are called to build the alternative community of God. We are not to eagerly await the world's destruction but rather to make visible the justice and compassion of God. When the healing and just ways of Jesus become visible through his community, the kingdom/community of God has drawn near, and Jesus makes his presence known.

In chapter two I explained that the Wi'am Conflict Resolution Centre in Bethlehem is planting a garden by the separation wall, and that their slogan is "No injustice will last forever." Pastor

Raheb espouses the same view in the way he interprets Matthew 5:5: "Blessed are the meek, for they shall inherit the land." They both see that injustice won't last forever. Empires look extremely powerful, but they fall. The community of love and the values of God's community will outlast them all.

With our partners around the world, we at Amos Trust have learned many lessons. We have seen Nicaragua come through a civil war. We have seen the witness of our partners there, the Council of Protestant Churches of Nicaragua or CEPAD, as they have created teams of volunteers to act as peace commissioners to heal the wounds of the conflict. We have seen them developing health care in the most inaccessible rural places (through their partner Amos Health and Hope). We have seen them fighting ecological problems by using simple agricultural methods to bring change. We have seen them (through their partner Prestanic) offering small loans, particularly to the women of the villages, so they can in turn create small businesses and start to make livelihoods.

We have seen Umthombo, in South Africa, campaign for ten years against the roundups of street children by the metro police. During these roundups the police would beat the children and take them miles outside of town whenever there were special events being held. For instance, when the conference against racism was held in Durban, the street children were taken to the bush, miles away, and separated at great risk to themselves. It would take them days to return, thus they would be invisible during that conference and similar events.

For ten years Umthombo campaigned, and then during the Street Child World Cup, which Umthombo hosted in 2010 before the Fifa World Cup, a final roundup was held. The roundup drew a lot of publicity because a British photographer from the *Sun* newspaper was arrested and taken to the police station along with one of my sons, and the *Sun* did a double-page spread on what was happening to the street children. The Durban municipality, which had asked for the roundups to stop, made sure thereafter that they did. So after years of campaigning to "treat street children better," now Umthombo and the municipality work together. Even the national government has looked at the policies Umthombo suggested for the right treatment of street children.

During the Street Child World Cup one of the teams came from a country that did not even acknowledge street children existed. But before the end of the tournament someone from the embassy of that country met with the children and applauded them.

In all of these situations the value of forgotten and oppressed people is being recognized. God's revolution of love is happening in quiet but distinctive ways. Seeds that have been sown for justice are bearing fruit.

We have seen Dalits in India campaign for their human rights, suffering enormously all kinds of abuse. Three thousand years of prejudice are not easily changed, but in Gomathimuthupuram, with our partners the Tamarind Tree Project, we have seen change coming. The project is committed to education as a way to break free from the chains that hold them back. We have seen people making a difference and more seeds being sown in God's revolution of love.

This revolution is happening (or is a possibility) all around the world. In church after church we need to reject systemic injustice because God loves justice. We have been called to strive first for the kingdom of God and God's justice. When we hunger and thirst for justice we will be satisfied because we understand that we are doing the tasks of the community of love.

So let the world be changed; let there be a place for everyone. We can campaign for this hope. Let's not be selfish in our worship or in our worship songs. Christianity is not just "me and Jesus," it is about community values. We can love God's world, looking after it and leaving it a safer place than when we first came to it. We can learn from the African concept of Ubuntu. We can care. We can be gentle, compassionate and concerned. We can go forth conscious that everybody is to be revered because they are created in God's image. We can make a difference, and when the work seems overwhelming we will be inspired by the fact that "no injustice can last forever" because God loves justice. God's revolution of love is on the move as we are the hands and feet of Jesus.

GOD OF THE PASSIONATE HEART

God of the passionate heart
Thank you for the values of your alternative community
They give us vocation
They show us causes
They show us the value of our neighbours
How to love one another
Why one person being treated unjustly matters
Because you are the God of the passionate heart
You are the God committed to the poor
We are in a world where they are forgotten as the rich get
        richer
You are the God who calls for purity of heart
You are the God who calls for action
For us to do justice and show mercy and walk humbly—
Thank you for the values of your alternative community
They give us our passion for life.
May we never lose our sense of calling.[12]

QUESTIONS FOR REFLECTION AND DISCUSSION

1. What does Archbishop Tutu mean when he says, "We need other human beings in order to be human"?

2. How do you understand the author's statement, "Separation, apartness and enmity . . . are the way of empire"?

3. The author says, "Jesus came with this very political message about a new alternative community—the kingdom of God. This is the message of hope. The gospel is good news for all, not just for a rich or powerful elite. This is why Christianity is such a dangerous, hopeful dream from God." Had you ever considered Christianity as "a dangerous, hopeful dream from God"? Discuss the implications of this sentence.

4. Ron Sider is quoted as saying that to follow Jesus "will mean transformed churches with a corporate lifestyle consistent with worship of the God of the poor. It will mean costly commitment to structural change in secular society." What would this mean for your worship community? Do you agree with Sider's fear that "the majority of affluent 'Christians' of all theological labels have bowed the knee to Mammon"? How would you recognize this in your own life and worship community?

5. Discuss practical ways that you or your worship community together could make Jesus' ways "become so visible, through his community, that people's lives are changed as they understand the humility and the impact of this healing and just way of life."

THE JUSTICE OF AMOS

Let justice roll down like waters,
and righteousness like an ever-flowing stream.

AMOS 5:24

Amos Trust is a small, creative Christian human rights agency that works with vibrant grassroots partners around the world. I founded Amos in 1985, and several people have asked me to write about the theology that informs and underpins Amos Trust.

Amos Trust is named after the words of the prophet Amos, especially Amos 5:24. Our first tagline was "For Jesus and His Justice," and then it became "Justice and Hope for the Forgotten," which it remains. With the word *forgotten* we are thinking of the powerless and the weak: so it could be street children, Dalits, Palestinians or the poor communities of Nicaragua. In time Amos may branch out to other areas of the world where many people are forgotten, ignored or simply dominated and oppressed, not least in our own societies.

When our previous chair of the trustees Beki Bateson wrote about Amos Trust in a newsletter at the time of our twenty-fifth anniversary, she said, "I've been privileged to be involved with this small, maverick, musical, punch-above-its-weight charity," and that says something about the nature of Amos Trust. Beki pointed out that Amos is committed, Amos is relational, Amos is creative, Amos listens and liberates.

It's a good summary. Relationships are at the heart of what we do. We have a passion for what we do. We try to express creativity in many ways, through design, writings, art, film, songs or music. And then Amos listens and liberates. We hope we listen carefully to what our partners are saying. Then we link arms with them in sharing the message they bring. Through them we help to be part of the journey toward liberation.

This helps us to journey toward our own liberation as we see our world differently. It helps us to deal with our own biases and prejudices. At the heart of Amos Trust is a spirituality that values and treasures each person as made "in the image of God." This helps us to stand with confidence on issues of human rights and justice. We are people of hope because there is a gospel of hope. We often call it our theology.

Amos Trust works particularly in four parts of the world now—in Durban, South Africa, among street children; in Nicaragua among poor communities; in Palestine and Israel with human rights groups, nonviolent activists and by supporting a hospital in Gaza; and in India among the Dalit community. We also worked previously in Uganda (educating AIDS orphans) and the Philippines (with street children and people living on a dump). In *Occupied Territories* I have talked about the lessons learned from our projects and our partners.

Amos was founded originally to support me in my role as a troubadour or storyteller addressing issues of justice and reconciliation. It enabled me to take up invitations where costs and expenses could not be met but where the opportunity was infinitely worthwhile. Amos has also been committed to my role of encouraging artists to develop art from a Christian viewpoint rooted in their own culture and not imperialized by Western values or style. Art and creativity is crucial to Amos Trust. Music has played a key part but so have design and other creative arts—even radical protests in art.

From the beginning Amos has sought to encourage those working against oppression and poverty around the world by building links with peacemakers in troubled situations. So originally Amos Trust was trying to tell the story and raise awareness of the different contexts of poverty, oppression and even conflict. But having made friends and understanding their stories, we decided to raise support for them. We started with the Taata Project in Uganda. This was founded by Bishop Misaeri Kauma, bishop of Namirembe at that time, and his wife, Geraldine. Through the years we have supported hundreds of children as they have gone through the education system from primary school to university. The importance of this is that they were almost all AIDS orphans and therefore would have ended up on the streets if it were not for Taata.

We then supported Mango Tree House in Manila, Philippines, which was a home for street children, and later we supported Cashew Tree School there as well, which was a school on the Payatas dumpsite. Gradually other projects were added in Nicaragua, South Africa, Palestine/Israel and India. On the campaigning side Amos particularly called for human rights for forgotten people or forgotten communities.

Because of these values Amos Trust has tried to reflect Jesus' words "blessed are the peacemakers" and "blessed are the merciful." Amos supports those committed to nonviolence and who support people who are caught up in poverty, injustice or oppression of any kind. We recognize we cannot cover every issue, so we first focused on six parts of the world, and now on four parts.

Sometimes people ask, "Wouldn't it be easier if you were linked only with one part of the world or one situation?" I believe the opposite is true. Amos benefits from not being a single-issue organization or focusing on a single part of the world. Though we do not have the diversity of a large NGO, we are able to build relationships and go into situations that give us diverse understandings. So we see the struggle, the pain, the constant emergency situations that arise in contexts such as the Palestine-Israel crisis; yet our focus on street children brings a simple but vital perspective on the value of those who are meant to be the future of our world. As we listen to friends and partners from different parts of the world we are encouraged and renewed in our understanding of justice, which comes back to our mutual understanding of the kingdom/community of God.

We are not called to only one task but to be a part of a community that makes visible justice, equality, healing and hope. This was illustrated when our current partners got together at Amos Trust's twenty-fifth celebration: "Let Justice Roll!" The Palestinians in attendance, for instance, were moved by listening to Dalit issues and shocked by the length of time of their oppression.

The street children that our partner Umthombo works with are on the streets because of poverty but also because of the lingering effects of apartheid. Injustice is behind the poverty still visible in the so-called townships of South Africa, and this poverty spills onto the streets. Rebuilding a community after a system like apartheid takes many years.

Our work in Nicaragua through CEPAD gives us models and examples of how to work with poor communities in rural areas through education, agriculture, health and peacemaking initiatives. These vital lessons are relevant around the world.

Our Influences and Partners

In chapter one I shared the story of when I heard Martin Luther King Jr., which has affected my thinking, my reading of the Bible and hopefully the way I live. Amos Trust's theology was also influenced by Archbishop Desmond Tutu, who offers a deep, challenging and joyful understanding of the Christian gospel. I was fortunate to be able to do an event with him with young people during apartheid time in South Africa. These young people had come from Soweto and other townships traumatized by the aggression of apartheid. To see how Archbishop Tutu helped to draw out the story from these people and to lead them through painful reminiscences until they came to a more hopeful and even joyful point was very special. Archbishop Tutu is a man of hope but a prophetic figure as well. Amos Trust has often been inspired by things that he has written and said.

Many others have influenced our thinking. For example, through our work in Palestine and Israel we have developed good relationships with Jewish and Muslim peacemakers as well as the Palestinian Christian community. They have deepened our understanding of injustice and how to counter it.

How do we choose our Amos partners? Relationships are key. When we meet people who have the same spirituality and motivation, the same commitment to justice, we know they are potential partners. We recognize that partnership is a two-way relationship, and we want people who will both motivate and challenge us on how justice should be lived out in their context. We bring our partners to Britain for our supporters to hear their views, and in turn we take trips with our supporters to see what our partners are doing on the ground.

We have always been committed to making sure when we are speaking for a community or for a group of people that our campaigning is based on the voices of our partners. We will not campaign unless we are reflecting the voice of our partners. So, for instance, if I am speaking at a demonstration about the situation in Palestine and Israel, I always quote our friends there because I feel I have no authority on my own. The view of those in that situation is of utmost importance, and their words and insights help us understand and campaign on their behalf.

Spirituality underpins Amos, which is exemplified by the various places where Amos has been based. For some time our offices were at St. Saviour's Church in Guildford, England, where I was on the staff, then for fifteen years we were at All Hallow's on the Wall in London, where I was guild vicar. Now we have moved to a new church, St. Clement's, Eastcheap, London, where the work of Amos is headed by our new director, the Reverend Chris Rose. I finished being the director of Amos Trust at the end of 2011 but remain in a part-time role with the title "founder."

It is inspiring to be based in a church where we can take time to pause and reflect our spirituality. We may participate in a liturgy, a time of silence, a time to light candles to symbolize our prayers, a time to listen to an update on a situation, a time to pray. For many years we had a service called "Wednesdays on the Wall," when we focused our prayers on our partners around the world. For a couple of years we held a similar service called "Thursdays at the Gate." It was held at the Westgate Chapel in the town of Lewes on the south coast of England. We recognize that in the quiet of these chapels we draw strength to continue our work as Christian activists and campaigners.

The following is an example of one of the prayers we used. This one is actually about Wednesdays on the Wall. It says something about the history and beauty of All Hallows on the Wall.

Everliving and everloving God—here on London Wall—
Where hundreds of years ago
Symon the Anker prayed and wrote 'The Fruyte of
    Redempcyion'—
Here where one hundred years ago
Samuel John Stone—hymn writer who wrote
'The Church's One Foundation,' wrote other hymns and
    poems—
Here as rector he prayed and cared
For the poorer workers of East London
And gave them shelter as they came into the City
Early to take advantage of cheaper trains.

Here in this beautiful but simple sacred space—
Praised by John Betjeman—
We have the humblest of services—
Yet we meet you in our liturgies
As we pray for those on our minds and in our hearts—
As we light our candles we place loved ones, friends,
    partners, peacemakers and communities around the
    world into your hands.
We pray for justice and peace—
And we give thanks for times of joy and hope.

So on Wednesdays we touch the holy
And in a simple moment of quiet meet with you
And somehow life comes into perspective again.
So thank you holy God for this sacred space of prayer.
Amen

Amos is fortunate to have long-term committed supporters. I
believe they stay with us because we reflect the values of the
kingdom of God. This is a theology that challenges empire, dom-

ination, injustice and inequality. It is a theology that reflects the
hope and joy of liberation. After twenty-five years of Amos
Trust, we held a special conference for our supporters and
brought our partners over to London from all the different
projects. It was a powerful and significant time. This prayer was
one written for that occasion.

Amos Prayer

O God we thank you for Amos Trust:
Thank you for partners who have inspired and challenged
    us;
Thank you for staff who have been so dedicated and
    committed;
Thank you for supporters who have given sacrificially—
Prayed without ceasing and campaigned passionately.

Together we have journeyed—learning from one
    another—
Seeing the strength of your loving and compassionate
    gospel
That brings down the mighty from their seats
And lifts up the lowly and forgotten.

Inspire us to go forward together, walking humbly with
    you,
Living your revolution of love—so justice will roll down
    like a river,
So that weapons will be turned into ploughshares
To bring community, hope, equality and dignity for all.
Amen

LET JUSTICE ROLL
Amos Trust Liturgies

In appendix one I mentioned the liturgies we used at "Wednesdays on the Wall" and "Thursdays at the Gate." These liturgies used at Amos Trust's twenty-fifth anniversary celebration give an idea of the kind of liturgies we use. Some of the prayers have been used in this book.

I have written most of them. Where that is not the case I have tried to give credit to the writers. Some prayers have been used so often we have forgotten where they came from, or we may have adapted them. If you recognize one that is not correctly credited, please let us know.

Justice and Peace for the Forgotten

Do Unto Others

Teach us to love your ways
And the values that make us whole
Teach us to love your ways
Then healing waters will flow
Teach us to love your ways
You're the God of the passionate heart

Teach us to love your ways
You are the God of the poor

So do unto others as you'd have them do to you
Do unto others as you'd have them do to you
Do unto others as you'd have them do to you
This is the way—the way of peace

Teach us to love your ways
To walk humbly and show mercy
Teach us to love your ways
To hunger for your justice
Teach us to love your ways
You're the God of the second chance
Teach us to love your ways
You're the God of the just heart

Teach us to love your ways
May we be pure in heart
Teach us to love the ones
Whom life and the world push down
Teach us to love your ways
Where there's no room for the law of revenge
For it's only wounded hands
That can reshape our world again

Do unto others as you'd have them do to you
Do unto others as you'd have them do to you
Do unto others as you'd have them do to you
This is the way—the way of peace
This is the way—the way of peace

The God Who Dances

LEADER Henri Matisse is rumoured to have said

That he'd only believe in a God

Who understood how to dance.

I believe you are the God of dance—

ALL **You are the God who moves in creation**

You are interwoven throughout evolution

You are the God who dances at dawn

You are the sparkle of light

You are the rhythm of life

Moving in mysterious ways

LEADER I feel you dancing on the earth

I sense your whisper in the trees

I breathe your spirit on the wind

ALL **You are the rhythm of life**

Moving in mysterious ways

LEADER But always dancing

You are the God who dances

Prayer About the Wall of Separation in a Land Once Called Holy

LEADER Living God, in Jesus you broke down the wall
of division

We see other walls that divide in our world.

Like the separation wall that cuts into the heart of Palestine,

Imprisoning a whole community—

Cutting them off from one another, from their work, from hospitals

From education and from places of worship.

ALL   **God of liberation strengthen them in their struggle**

May hope be born again in Bethlehem, the birthplace of the Prince of Peace

And throughout this land once called holy.

LEADER   May Palestinians find justice at last,

So Palestine and Israel can both live in peace—

Both live securely—both live in freedom

Without walls, without checkpoints, closures and curfews.

ALL   **May we realize the great message of hope that all are chosen or none,**

We're all in this together—

One God, one community, one hope, one future.

God of Justice

God of all times and places,
Who brings light into the world's darkness,
We come to you with our prayers:

So that the children may no longer be denied education;
So that the sick may no longer die from curable diseases;
So that the workers may no longer be cheated of justice;
Your kingdom come:
Your will be done on earth as it is in heaven.

So that financial systems may no more burden the poorest;
So that our trade may no longer deny a fair wage;
So that debt may no more trap nations in poverty;
Your kingdom come:
Your will be done on earth as it is in heaven.

So that the innocent will walk free from prison;
So that minorities will live without fear;
So that the whole earth will worship in freedom;
Your kingdom come:
Your will be done on earth as it is in heaven.

So that the Palestinians may find a home;
So that the Dalits will be allowed their dignity;
So that children will know they are loved and valued;
So that the poor and marginalized will discover their worth
    in the eyes of God and in the eyes of God's community;
So that racism and oppression may be banished from the
    earth;
Your kingdom come:
Your will be done on earth as it is in heaven.
Peter Greystone; additional verse by Garth Hewitt[1]

Holy Ground

Go gently, my friends;
Feel the good earth
Beneath your feet,
Celebrate the rising of the sun,
Listen to the birds at dawn.
Walk gently under
The silent stars,
Knowing you are on holy ground,
Held in love—
In the wonder of God's creation.[2]

Prayer

LEADER   God of community and compassion,

            We take a moment to look round the world

            At the needs of those who do not have enough
            to eat—

            And those who cannot break the chains of
            poverty

            Those who try to survive on the streets of the
            cities of our world.

ALL   **We pray for politicians that they will
            remember**

            The weak and the vulnerable,

            **For those who work to bring hope to the
            vulnerable—**

            **For campaigners, and those who give and
            those who pray.**

LEADER   Gustavo Gutiérrez said "Woe to those the Lord finds dry eyed";

Keep our hearts warm Lord and our vision clear and simple.

ALL   **May we play our part in the healing of the worldwide community;**

It may seem such a small part,

But it is something beautiful for God.

So may we serve you in our lives and in our world

In the name of God—the compassionate—the merciful—and the just.

Amen.

THE VALUE OF A HUMAN BEING

Prayer for South African Street Children

LEADER   Compassionate God

May we be those who listen to the voices of the forgotten generation—

The children on the streets of South Africa.

Day by day they face the challenges of abuse, hunger, trauma,

Always asking "will anyone care for me?"

ALL   **God of mercy and justice, may we reach out in love,**

As we remember that each day is a battle—

Each day is a struggle to survive.

Bless the work of those who walk beside them,

As they seek daily to bring strength, dignity

And hope for those forgotten children.

LEADER   May the children of the streets—walking the road to crucifixion—

Find the way to resurrection—

ALL   Because we listen, because we support them,

And because we bring your holy and active love.

We ask in the name of Jesus

Who said, "Let the children come to me."

GOD'S REVOLUTION OF LOVE

Song: God's Revolution of Love (see the lyrics in chap. 6)

LEADER   It is not true that we must accept inhumanity and discrimination, hunger and poverty, death and destruction.

ALL   This is true: I have come that they may have life and have it abundantly.

LEADER	It is not true that we are simply victims of the powers of evil that seek to rule the world.
ALL	**This is true: to me is given all authority in heaven and on earth, and lo, I am with you always, even to the end of the age.**
LEADER	It is not true that we have to wait for those who are specially gifted, who are the prophets of the church, before we can do anything.
ALL	**This is true: I will pour out my spirit on all flesh, and your sons and your daughters will prophesy, and your old men shall dream dreams and your young men shall see visions.**
LEADER	It is not true that our dreams for the liberation of humankind and our dreams for justice, human dignity, or peace are not meant for this earth and for this history.
ALL	**This is true: the year comes and it is now, that true worshippers shall worship the Father in spirit and in truth.**[3]

Readings

Love your enemies, do good to those who hate you, bless those who curse you, pray for those who abuse you. If anyone strikes you on the cheek, offer the other also; and from anyone who takes away your coat, do not withhold even your shirt. . . . Do to others as you would have them do to you. (Luke 6:27-29, 31)

Is not this the fast that I choose:
   to loose the bonds of injustice,
   to undo the thongs of the yoke,
to let the oppressed go free
   and to break every yoke?
Is it not to share your bread with the hungry
   and bring the homeless poor into your house. . . .
Then your light shall break forth like the dawn,
   and your healing shall spring up quickly. (Isaiah 58:6-8)

Quote from Tom Hewitt

With the right city wide strategy and philosophy we are coming to see that the urban phenomenon of street children can be transformed in Durban. Ours is an ambitious revolution. We believe that the best way to address the problem of street children is to listen to them. As Paulo Freire the Brazilian philosopher of education said, "Who better prepared than the oppressed to understand the terrible significance of an oppressive society."

Listening in this context is not a simple act. Street children are an oppressed group who have been told through actions and sometimes words that they are the rubbish of society. Little wonder then that they internalize this and learn to see themselves as somehow inferior, and worse still, the architects of their own misery. Can the street children really imagine they are made in the image of God? Could they possibly imagine that they know things that are crucial to the development of new strategies in the liberation of street children? We believe so.[4]

Reflection on Creative Extremists

But though I was initially disappointed at being categorized as an extremist, as I continued to think about the matter I gradually gained a measure of satisfaction from the label. Was not Jesus an extremist for love: "Love your enemies, bless them that curse you, do good to them that hate you, and pray for them which spitefully use you, and persecute you." Was not Amos an extremist for justice: "Let justice roll down like waters and righteousness like an ever-flowing stream." Was not Paul an extremist for the Christian gospel: "I bear in my body the marks of the Lord Jesus." Was not Martin Luther an extremist: "Here I stand; I cannot do otherwise, so help me God." And John Bunyan: "I will stay in jail to the end of my days before I make a butchery of my conscience." And Abraham Lincoln: "This nation cannot survive half slave and half free." And Thomas Jefferson: "We hold these truths to be self-evident, that all men are created equal . . ." So the question is not whether we will be extremists, but what kind of extremists will we be. Will we be extremists for hate or for love? Will we be extremists for the preservation of injustice or for the extension of justice?[5]

The Rebel and the Revolutionary

A rebel hates
A revolutionary loves
A rebel hates injustice
A revolutionary loves justice
A rebel negates
A revolutionary creates
A rebel reacts
A revolutionary acts

A rebel divides
A revolutionary unites
A rebel says: "my rights"
A revolutionary: "our duties"

A rebel attacks
the singer
And is deaf to the song
A revolutionary retrains
the singer
And rewrites the song

A rebel sees red
All vision blinkered
By the burning grass
A revolutionary sees
The wondrous colours
That is the rainbow
Which follows the deluge
Which quells the flames

For a revolutionary knows
Where promises lie
When hopes are false
How rage is disciplined
Why the grass has roots

A rebel asks *"why?"*
A revolutionary, *"why not?"*
A rebel perceives
The winter
Of today
A revolutionary conceives
The spring
For tomorrow

For tomorrow shall dawn
Dreams will come true
The nightmare will end
When a rebel
Matures
Into a revolutionary[6]

Dalit Prayer

God of all places and this place: you promised a new earth
where the hungry will feast and the oppressed go free.
Come Lord, build that place among us.

God of all times and this time: you promised a new day
when the fearful will laugh and the sick find healing. **Come
Lord, speed that time among us.**

God of all people, our God: take what we have and what
we hope for, make this a world where the poor find good
news. **We come Lord, to share in the work of your
kingdom, until the new earth is created among us.
Amen.**

God of all, it's so hard to live on the margins—lonely and
forgotten, despised . . . dependent . . . Remember me, put
back my confidence, restore my dignity and walk down the
edges with me . . . Then knowing you Lord, I shall rise . . .
rise in hope.[7]

Make a Difference in the World

May God bless you with discomfort at easy answers,
Half-truths, superficial relationships,
So that you will live deep within your heart.

May God bless you with anger at injustice,
Oppression and exploitation of people,
So that you will work for justice, equity and peace.

May God bless you with tears to shed for those who
    suffer from pain,
Rejection, starvation and war,
So that you will reach out your hand to comfort them and
    change their pain to joy.

And may God bless you with the foolishness to think that
    you can make a difference to the world,
So that you will do the things which others tell you
    cannot be done.[8]

REFLECTION: "GOD'S DREAM," ARCHBISHOP DESMOND TUTU

LEADER   Dear child of God, before we can become
          God's partners, we must know what God
          wants for us. "I have a dream," God says.
          "Please help Me to realise it:

ALL   **"It is a dream of a world whose ugliness and
          squalor and poverty, its war and hostility,
          its greed and harsh competitiveness, its
          alienation and disharmony are changed
          into their glorious counterparts.**

LEADER   "It is a dream where there will be more
          laughter, joy and peace, more justice and
          goodness and compassion and love and caring
          and sharing.

ALL   "I have a dream that swords will be beaten
          into ploughshares, spears into pruning
          hooks. My children will know they are
          members of one family, the human family,
          God's family, My family. In God's family
          there are no outsiders . . . all belong."[9]

Prayer for Forgiveness

ALL   O God you see our motives and the desires
          of our hearts.

          Forgive us for the mistakes we have made—

          Forgive us for the wrong we have done—

          Forgive us for walking the wrong way—

LEADER   For not empathizing with that person—

          For reacting too strongly.

          Mistakes and failure make us feel we have lost
          our dignity.

ALL   Restore our souls—make us whole

          Give us back the spring in our steps

          The lightness in our hearts

          So we can bring hope and show love to
          others

          And make good where we have made
          mistakes.

LEADER   You are the God of second chances

Walk with us on the road back

To wholeness and dignity

To loving our neighbor and loving ourself

And loving you with all our heart and soul.

The Feast of Life

All shall be included in the Feast of Life
All shall be included in the Feast of Life
All shall be included in the Feast of Life
Good news from the Lord.

Chorus: *Good news for the poor*
Good news from the Lord
A new world is coming—
The time is at hand
Good news from the Lord

Hand in hand together we will work for peace
Hand in hand together we will work for the least
Hand in hand together all at the feast
Good news from the Lord

Chorus: Good news . . .

A voice in the desert cries out for the Lord
A voice in the desert says straighten the road
A voice cries out make the rough places smooth
Prepare the way of the Lord

Chorus: Good news . . .

Valleys will be filled in and mountains brought low
God takes the powerful from off of their thrones
Lifts up the lowly and the hungry are fed
Good news from the Lord

Chorus: Good news . . .

KAIROS PALESTINE
A Moment of Truth

The following is an approved abridgement of Kairos Palestine: A Moment of Truth issued by Palestinian Christians in December 2009.[1]

We, a group of Christian Palestinians, after prayer, reflection and an exchange of opinion, cry out from within the suffering in our country under Israeli occupation, with a cry of hope in the absence of all hope.

The reality on the ground is one of the Israeli occupation, and all that results from this situation: the dehumanizing effect of the separation wall; the effect of the Israeli settlements that ravage our land in the name of God and of force; humiliation at checkpoints; restrictions on religious liberty; and the suffering of Jerusalem where homes are being demolished or expropriated.

There is also the reality of the refugees, waiting for their rights to be realised, as well as the Palestinians who are citizens of Israel waiting to enjoy equality.

Young people, both Muslim and Christian, are emigrating in this absence of hope. The shrinking number of Christians is a dangerous consequence of the continued conflict.

We believe that the Word of God is a living Word, casting a

particular light on each period of history, manifesting to Christian believers what God is saying to us here and now.

We know that certain theologians in the West try to attach a biblical legitimacy to the infringement of our rights. We declare that the Israeli occupation of Palestinian land is a sin against God and humanity because it deprives the Palestinians of their basic human rights.

The mission of the Church is prophetic, to speak the Word of God courageously, honestly and lovingly in the local context and in the midst of daily events. We say that our option as Christians in the face of the Israeli occupation is to resist. But it is resistance with love as its logic. It is thus a creative resistance for it must find human ways that engage the humanity of the enemy.

Our numbers are few but our message is great and important. Our land is in urgent need of love. Our love is a message to the Muslim and to the Jew, as well as to the world.

Our word to the Churches of the world is firstly a word of gratitude for the solidarity you have shown toward us in word, deed and presence among us. It is also a call to repentance and to revisit fundamentalist theological positions that support certain unjust political options with regard to the Palestinian people.

Our question to our brothers and sisters in the Churches today is: Are you able to help us get our freedom back? For this is the only way you can help the two peoples attain justice, peace, security and love. In order to understand our reality, we say to the Churches: Come and see. You will know the facts and the people of this land, Palestinians and Israelis alike.

We condemn all forms of racism, whether religious or ethnic, including anti-Semitism and Islamophobia, and we call on you to condemn it and oppose it in all its manifestations. We call on you to take a position of truth with regards to Israel's occupation of Palestinian land. We see boycott and divestment as non-violent tools for justice, peace and security for all.

Our word to the international community is to stop the double-standards, and insist on the international resolutions regarding the Palestinian problem with regard to all parties.

To Palestinians and Israelis: our appeal is to reach a common vision, built on equality and sharing, not on superiority, negation of the other or aggression, using the pretext of fear and security. Let the state be a state for all its citizens, with a vision constructed on respect for religion but also equality, justice, liberty and respect for pluralism and not on domination by a religion or a numerical majority.

LET JUSTICE ROLL DOWN LIKE WATER
A Study on the Prophet Amos

The following is a study on the prophet Amos written especially for this book by Rev. Dr. Jasmine Devadason, theologian, Dalit voice and Amos Trust partner from Tamil Nadu, India.

One of the important messages in the Bible is God's concern for a just society. Israelite law sets out principles of fairness, equality and social justice which reflected the Israelites' understanding of herself as a people redeemed from oppression. The Torah embodied a vision of social righteousness. In the covenant made with God Israel had promised to reflect God's justice, mercy, love and righteousness. The covenant meant they would act as ambassadors of Yahweh, and as a covenant people they were to set the standards of truth and justice and all that is dear to God, thus setting them apart from the nations. So justice is an important aspect in the life of God's people. When there is no justice in the society as God expected, then God intervenes either directly or through mediators such as prophets. Eighth-century prophets (Isaiah, Amos, Micah and Hosea) were good examples of this, and they were prophesizing against the injustice that prevailed in their context. Amos in particular emphasized the need for justice in the society. The whole book of Amos is about justice. The context in which Amos prophesied is similar to our international context where there is still poverty, division and social discrimination and need for justice.

CONTEXT OF AMOS

Amos prophesied in a time of prosperity in Israel. In the first half of the eighth century both Judah and Israel had enjoyed a time of great prosperity and had attained the highest political power. This kind of prosperity and political power paved the way to injustice and oppression in society. The presence of injustice among the eighth-century community was clearly expressed in the prophetical books. There were sharp divisions between rich and poor. The rich became richer by oppressing the poor, who became poorer. The original owners lost their homes while the corrupt and the rich became the owners.

Even the government was corrupt, and the covetous judiciary system made life miserable for the poor of the land. The injustice that the poor people suffered was due not only to the corruption of the court officials but also to the way in which the legal assembly in Israel was constituted. Those who participated in the assembly "at the gate" were the elders of the community, and it is probable that these consisted of the senior male members of every household. Indeed, it would appear that the status of an "elder" was contingent upon possession of house and property, and if this was the case then it is clear that the legal assemblies could only have functioned properly while the citizens remained free, land-owning householders. Dispossession of property would therefore have entailed a loss of representation in the local assembly, and it is possible that Isaiah's concern for justice is to be directly related to his denunciation of those who evicted the poorer citizens from their smallholdings.

The most important issue it highlights is the conduct of many members of the ruling class who attempt to gain more and more land-property for enlarging the large estate business. This led to the small peasants losing their freedom, and being sold as debt-slaves (bonded laborers).

The growth of economic property during the period of Uzziah due to the tribute and trade income received by the nation caused a rapid shift of property and ownership. The original landowners lost their land, which made the majority of the people's living conditions miserable. Beneficiaries of the growth were the ruling class and the elite, who dominated the state in a mercenary way. Isaiah 5:8-10 reflects the growth of large estates through *Latifundialization* (the process of land accumulation in the hands of a small, wealthy elite to the deprivation of the peasantry). This kind of change and growth brought a new urban society and also a social aristocracy.

In this time of history God called Amos to prophesy against the injustices and to tell of the judgment of the Lord against the nations.

Amos's View of Justice

God's people were required as part of the covenant to show mercy and help the poor and oppressed. They were required to create a socially just society according to what God had commanded them.

Amos connects justice with life—where Israel does not practice justice, the community declines. To have life in the community, justice and righteousness must roll down like a river after the winter rains, and persevere like those few streams that remain the same even during the summer drought. For Amos justice is not an abstract concept but it is a life-giving power. So the importance of justice is a main thrust in the book of Amos, which is relevant for today's context.

Two examples for reflection—

Amos 8

Hear this, you that trample on the needy,
　　and bring to ruin the poor of the land,
saying, "When will the new moon be over
　　so that we may sell grain;
and the sabbath,
　　so that we may offer wheat for sale?
We will make the ephah small and the shekel great,
　　and practise deceit with false balances,
buying the poor for silver
　　and the needy for a pair of sandals,
　　and selling the sweepings of the wheat." [Amos 8:4-6]

In this passage Amos is condemning the business practices of his day [Amos 8:5-6]. Because the traders use corrupt scales, which discriminated against the producers [verse 5b]. Prices were inflated: the powerful received profits while the poor received less than they deserved [verse 5b]. Poor producers were not treated as humans [verse 6a] and they even sold the poor and the needy for a pair of sandals. (There was a lack of concern for quality [verse 6b].)

It is all about the need for justice in trade, the need to pay workers fairly and not exploit them to make money.

Trading/marketing had become the major part of the life of the rich. The rich businessmen of the day were saying, "When will the New Moon be over that we may sell grain, and the Sabbath be ended that we may market wheat?" [verse 5a] so that they could gain wealth by exploiting the poor.

A similar situation exists today. Although the global economy as a whole has grown over the last twenty years, the economies of many poor countries have actually shrunk. While their share of world trade is tiny, trade for individual poor countries is actually a far more significant contributor to their national income than for most rich countries. Nearly a third of Africa's income is accounted for by trade—a much higher proportion than for Europe or the USA. This means that the impact of international trade rules and policies tends to be far greater on poor countries than rich countries.

International trade today does not work for the poor, but it could play an important role, if paid fairly, which can offer people living in poverty the dignity of a just reward for their labor. However, the reality of mainstream trade is that it is rife with exploitation.

In this context what is our responsibility?

"Are you not like Cushites to me?" says Yahweh. "Did I not bring Israel up from the land of Egypt, the Philistines from Caphtor, and Aram from Qir?" (Amos 9:7)

Amos 9:7-10 introduces messages that contradict the popular belief that Israel occupies a special place because of its exodus from Egypt, and therefore is exempt from judgment of God.

Firstly, God declares that the Israelites are just like Ethiopians who are from a distant land. Secondly, Israel is equated with her close foes the Philistines and Arameans. God not only brought Israel out of Egypt, but the Philistines out of Captor and Arameans from Qir. Both the Philistines and Arameans experienced their own exoduses. Here Amos is making a clear point about how God deals with different groups of people.

Their election is connected with a greater responsibility; here it is dissociated from all privileges over against other people. So the other nations also have a history of salvation, even if they are unaware of it and Israel does not recognize it, their migrations, too, are to be seen in the context of the saving plan of God.

God's involvement in history is apparent here—the exodus from Egypt is listed along with the migration of the Philistines and Arameans, and therefore put on the same footing. While the prophet confirms the basic faith of Israel is the liberation of Israelites from Egypt, he also adds to that the liberation of other people. This basic affirmation of Yahweh's historical relationship with Israel is neither denied nor robbed by the expansion to include the Philistines and Arameans. What it denied is the theology based on that faith that Yahweh's act in the exodus established Israel in a special status vis-à-vis the other nations. The exodus is set in the context of international history and becomes in this context a manifestation of Yahweh's unconditional sovereignty.

The religious claim of choseness does not make any difference between the Israelites and other nations, but it is based on the act of establishing justice in the society that makes special people. The emphasis here is that Yahweh is God of justice, and wherever people are oppressed because of injustice he takes sides with the poor and liberates them from oppression.

Today battles and civil unrest continue to rage in various parts of the world. The environment is facing increasing threats; people in different parts of the world fight in the name of religion. The religious life becomes miserable—people start worshipping the gods of money, power and material success, and there is no place for God.

Religion, which is meant to be for human salvation and a source of unity, has been a divisive force. We live in a world today that needs to hear the faith proclaimed by Amos, faith in a different way and new day coming, faith in a broader picture than the one we can see. We need a faith that brings us together irrespective of religion/race/culture, faith that helps us to acknowledge the differences, faith that pulls us out of ourselves and into a passionate concern for the whole creation.

To summarize my summary:

1. Context is similar to today's international context.

2. Social injustice (which could be compared with the Dalits situation in India).

3. Corrupt trading systems (which could be compared with the situation in Nicaragua and other African countries and how they are affected by the International trade policies).

4. God who cares for oppressed irrespective of their religion/ race/context (which could be compared with the situation in Palestine).

5. What is our responsibility? Working towards just society? Taking the role of Amos to condemn injustice?

NOTES

Chapter 1: God Loves Justice

[1]Martin Luther King Jr., "The Three Dimensions of a Complete Life," address at St. Paul's Cathedral, London, 1964; as quoted in Garth Hewitt and Martin Wroe, *Nero's Watching Video* (London: Hodder & Stoughton, 1987), p. 20.

[2]Misa campesina nicarguense/Nicaraguan Peasant Mass, by Carlos Mejia Godoy, translated by Dinah Livingstone, 3rd revised bilingual edition published by Nicaragua Solidarity Campaign, London 2007. Used by permission.

[3]Gustavo Parajon, interview by Garth Hewitt for Amos Trust film *God Loves Justice*, 2010.

Chapter 2: Bethlehem Is Calling

[1]Michael Moore, *Capitalism: A Love Story*, cited in "Michael Moore Capitalism Quotes," We the People for Peace, accessed February 4, 2014, www.wethepeopleforpeace.org/upload/MichaelMooreCapitalismQuotes.pdf.

[2]Jasmine Devadason, a Dalit theologian, has written this specifically for the book at my request. A fuller explanation by Jasmine is found in appendix 3.

[3] Mitri Raheb, *I Am a Palestinian Christian* (Minneapolis: Fortress Press, 1995), p. 14.

[4]Sami Awad, executive director of Holy Land Trust, interview by Garth Hewitt, 2013.

[5]Martin Luther King Jr., *Where Do We Go from Here: Chaos or Community?* (Boston: Beacon Press, 2010), pp. 64-65.

[6]Thomas Merton, *A Book of Hours* (Notre Dame, IN: Sorin, 2007), p. 124.

[7]Mazin Qumsiyeh, interview by Garth Hewitt, Bethlehem, June 2012.

[8]Zoughbi Zoughbi, director of Wi'am Conflict Resolution Centre, Christmas message, December 2012. Used with permission.

[9]Sami Awad, executive director of Holy Land Trust, interview by Garth Hewitt, 2013.

Chapter 3: Be the Hands of Jesus

[1]M. Scott Peck, *What Return Can I Make?* (New York: Simon & Schuster, 1985), pp. 52-53.

[2]Arvind P. Nirmal, "From No People to God's People" (Madras: Department of Dalit Theology, 1989).

[3]Column 1 in "The Rule of the Congregation (Messianic Rule)," Dead Sea Scrolls.

[4]Kenneth E. Bailey, *Jesus Through Middle Eastern Eyes* (Downers Grove, IL: IVP Academic, 2008), p. 311.

[5]Marcus J. Borg and N. T. Wright, *The Meaning of Jesus: Two Visions* (New York: HarperCollins, 2000), p. 38.

[6]Josephus, quoted in ibid.

[7]Elias Chacour, as quoted in Garth Hewitt, *Pilgrims and Peacemakers* (Abingdon, UK: The Bible Reading Fellowship, 1995), p. 74.

[8]Ibid., p. 7.

[9]Ched Myers, *Binding the Strong Man: A Political Reading of Mark's Story of Jesus*, 20th anniv. ed. (Maryknoll, NY: Orbis, 2008), p. 294.

[10]William Herzog, *Jesus, Justice and the Reign of God* (Louisville: Westminster John Knox, 2000), p. 142.

[11]Ibid., p. 143.

[12]Ibid.

[13]Nive Hall, Amos Trust, April 2013, used with permission.

[14]Nirmal, "From No People to God's People."

[15]Naim Ateek, Sabeel Liberation Theology Group, Easter letter, 2012.

[16]Gyles Brandreth, "My Idea of Heaven," *The Telegraph*, April 27, 2001, www.telegraph.co.uk/culture/4723136/My-idea-of-Heaven.html.

[17]Walter Wink, "Facing the Myth of Redemptive Violence," *Ekklesia*, May 21, 2012, www.ekklesia.co.uk/content/cpt/article_060823wink.shtml.

[18]Desmond Tutu, quoted in Gary Younge, "The Secrets of a Peacemaker," *The Guardian*, May 22, 2009, www.theguardian.com/books/2009/may/23/interview-desmond-tutu.

CHAPTER 4: TIME FOR ACTION

[1]"Gaza Strip: Operation Cast Lead, 27 Dec. '08 to 18 Jan. '09," *B'Tselem*, January 1, 2011, www.btselem.org/gaza_strip/castlead_operation. B'Tselem is the Israeli information center for human rights.

[2]"A Moment of Truth: A Word of Faith, Hope and Love from the Heart of Palestinian Suffering," World Council of Churches, December 11, 2009, www.oikoumene.org/en/resources/documents/other-ecumenical-bodies/kairos-palestine-document.

[3]"Time for Action," Kairos Britain, www.kairosbritain.org.uk/resources/documents/Time-for-Action/Time-for-Action.pdf.

[4]"A Moment of Truth," 4.2.1.

[5]"The Five Marks of Mission," Anglican Communion, www.anglican
communion.org/ministry/mission/fivemarks.cfm.

[6]Naim Ateek, interview by Garth Hewitt, 2013.

[7]Ibid.

[8]Ibid.

[9]Garth Hewitt, *Making Holy Dreams Come True* (London: SPCK, 2006),
p. 23.

CHAPTER 5: MONEY, WAR AND EQUALITY

[1]Andrew Sullivan, "Barack Obama's Debate Implosion Raises the
Stakes," *The Sunday Times*, October 14, 2012, www.theaustralian.com
.au/news/world/barack-obamas-debate-implosion-raises-the-stakes/
story-fnb64oi6-1226495625580#.

[2]Alan Wolfe, "The Ridiculous Rise of Ayn Rand," *The Chronicle of Higher
Education*, August 19, 2012, http://chronicle.com/blogs/conversation/2012/
08/19/the-ridiculous-rise-of-ayn-rand.

[3]Abraham Heschel, "Existence and Celebration," in *Moral Grandeur and
Spiritual Audacity*, ed. Susannah Heschel (New York: Farrar, Straus &
Giroux, 1997), pp. 31-32.

[4]Aditya Chakrabortty, "An Action-Packed Thriller Is About to Unfold in
Davos, Switzerland," *Guardian*, January 21, 2013,www.theguardian.com/
commentisfree/2013/jan/21/davos-switzerland-rich-plotting-richer.

[5]John Ruskin, quoted in Bernadette Meaden, "There Is No Wealth but
Life," *Ekklesia*, July 3, 2012, www.ekklesia.co.ik/node/16804.

[6]Helena Kennedy, "Serve 'Em Right," *Third Way*, January-February 2013,
www.thirdwaymagazine.co.uk/editions/janfeb-2013/high-profile/
serve-'em-right.aspx.

[7]Quoted in Lizzy Davies, "Pope Condemns Idolatry of Cash in Capitalism,"
The Guardian, September 22, 2013, www.theguardian.com/world/2013/
sep/22/pope-francis-idol-money.

[8]Cornel West, "Cornel West Exposes Obama Hypocrisy," *World News Daily*,
January 22, 2013, www.informationclearinghouse.info/article33682.htm.

[9]Gustavo Parajon, quoted in *God Loves Justice*, a film by the Amos
Trust, 2010.

[10]John Dear, "What Jesus Taught in the Garden of Gethsemane," *National
Catholic Reporter*, March 13, 2012, http://ncronline.org/blogs/road-peace/
what-jesus-taught-garden-gethsemane.

[11]Hillel the Elder, Babylonian Talmud, tractate *Šabbat* 3a.

[12]Cornel West, quoted in Andrew Goldman, "Cornel West Flunks the
President," *New York Times*, July 22, 2011, www.nytimes.com/2011/07/24/
magazine/talk-cornel-west.html.

[13]Simon Jenkins, "Drones Are Fool's Gold: They Prolong Wars We Can't Win," *Guardian*, January 10, 2013, www.theguardian.com/commentisfree/2013/jan/10/drones-fools-gold-prolong-wars.

[14]"DSEI Guest List Reveals Government Will Host Dictators at Arms Fair," Campaign Against Arms Trade, September 9, 2013, www.caat.org.uk/media/press-releases/2013-09-09.php.

[15]Sarah Waldron, quoted in ibid.

[16]"Christians Plan 'Exorcism' at London Arms Fair," *Ekklesia*, September 6, 2013, www.ekklesia.co.uk/node/19009.

[17]Vijay Mehta, *The Economics of Killing: How the West Fuels War and Poverty in the Developing World* (London: Pluto Press, 2012), p. 163.

[18]Desmond Tutu, address at Lancing College, Sussex, England, May 22, 2007.

[19]See, for instance, Kate Pickett and Richard Wilkinson, *The Spirit Level: Why Greater Equality Makes Societies Stronger* (New York: Bloomsbury, 2009).

[20]Oxfam, "The Cost of Inequality: How Wealth and Income Extremes Hurt Us All," Oxfam.org, January 18, 2013, www.oxfam.org/sites/www.oxfam.org/files/cost-of-inequality-oxfam-mb180113.pdf.

[21]Garth Hewitt, *Holy Dreams to Feed the Soul* (London: SPCK, 2007), p. 12.

[22]Dwight D. Eisenhower, "The Chance for Peace," speech, April 16, 1953, www.edchange.org/multicultural/speeches/ike_chance_for_peace.html.

[23]Chris Howson and Keith Hebden, "Liturgy of Exorcism and Repentance," Christianity Uncut, September 7, 2013, http://christianityuncut.wordpress.com/2013/09/07/liturgy-of-exorcism-and-repentance.

Chapter 6: God's Revolution of Love

[1]Archbishop Desmond Tutu, address delivered at Morehouse Medical School Commencement, May 15, 1993, quoted in Michael Battle, *Ubuntu: I in You and You in Me* (New York: Seabury, 2009), p. 54.

[2]Naim Ateek, Cedar Duaybis, and Maurine Tobin, *Challenging Empire* (Jerusalem: Sabeel Ecumenical Liberation Theology Center, 2012), p. 194.

[3]Ibid.

[4]Mitri Raheb, "Blessed Are the Meek," in *Challenging Empire: God, Faithfulness and Resistance*, ed. Naim Ateek, Cedar Duaybis and Maurine Tobin (Jerusalem: Sabeel Ecumenical Liberation Theology Center, 2012), p. 54.

[5]Ibid.

[6]Peter West and Mary West, *For Where Your Treasure Is: What the Bible Says About Wealth* (Wymington, UK: Meeting Place, n.d.), www.themeeting

placewymington.co.uk/images/treasure.pdf.

[7]Ronald J. Sider, *Rich Christians in an Age of Hunger*, 1st ed. (Downers Grove, IL: InterVarsity Press, 1978), p. 225.

[8]E. F. Schumacher, *Small Is Beautiful: A Study of Economics as If People Mattered* (London: Abacus, 1978), p. 290.

[9]Helena Kennedy, "Serve 'Em Right," *Third Way*, January-February 2013, www.thirdwaymagazine.co.uk/editions/janfeb-2013/high-profile/serve-'em-right.aspx.

[10]Michael Moore, London, March 10, 2003.

[11]Quoted in Battle, *Ubuntu*, pp. 58-59.

[12]Garth Hewitt, *Holy Dreams to Feed the Soul* (London: SPCK, 2007), p. 15.

APPENDIX 2: LET JUSTICE ROLL

[1]Peter Greystone, additional verse by Garth Hewitt, "God of Justice," in *A World of Blessing*, compiled by Geoffrey Duncan (Norwich, UK: Canterbury Press, 2000), p. 110.

[2]Peter Millar, "Holy Ground," *The Surprise of the Sacred: Finding God in Unexpected Places* (Norwich, UK: Canterbury Press, 2011).

[3]Allan Boesak, *Imaging the Word: An Arts and Lectionary Resource*, vol. 2 (Cleveland, OH: United Church Press, 1995).

[4]Tom Hewitt, "A Revolutionary Goal," *ThirdWay*, June 2010, www.thirdwaymagazine.co.uk/editions/june-2010/features/a-revolutionary-goal.aspx.

[5]Martin Luther King Jr., "Letter from Birmingham Jail," April 16, 1963.

[6]Francis Khoo, "The Rebel and the Revolutionary," in *Our Thoughts Are Free*, ed. Tan Jing Quee, Teo Soh Lung, and Koh Kay Yew (Singapore: Ethos, 2009).

[7]A Dalit Prayer, Church of South India Diaconal Ministry, 2002.

[8]Source unknown, "Make a Difference in the World," in *A World of Blessing*, compiled by Geoffrey Duncan (Norwich, UK: Canterbury Press, 2000), p. 102.

[9]Adapted from Desmond Tutu, *God Has a Dream* (London: Rider Press, 2004), p. 19.

APPENDIX 3: KAIROS PALESTINE

[1]Used by permission. The full Kairos Palestine document is available at www.kairospalestine.ps.

ABOUT THE AUTHOR

 **Garth Hewitt**—troubadour, gospel singer, protest singer and activist—released his first album in 1973 and his most recent, *Something for the Soul,* in 2014, with more than forty albums in between. Garth's rootsy storytelling songs are influenced by country, folk and blues. In 1988 he received the International Artist Award from the Gospel Music Association in Nashville, Tennessee—though he couldn't be there that night as he was playing in Gdansk, Poland.

Touring tirelessly for forty years, Garth has visited areas of poverty, conflict, deprivation and disaster, prioritizing friendships with local people and bringing them encouragement. He always returns to Europe and the United States with personal stories, bringing to life media headlines, keeping individuals' stories at the forefront when newspapers have forgotten them, and challenging the privileged to share and to join the protest against injustice.

Garth founded the human rights charity Amos Trust in 1985, worked for twenty-six years as its director and currently maintains a role as founder. He now also works in collaboration with The Garth Hewitt Foundation and GingerDog Records to continue writing and making his resources available. Garth's latest album, *Something for the Soul,* is a musical companion to this book. The songs reflect prayers, songs of hope, stories and Bethlehem theology.

Garth has written nine previous books, including several books of meditations and prayers.

For fifteen years Garth was Guild Vicar of All Hallows on the Wall in the City of London, where Amos Trust was based. He is now associate priest of St Clement's, Eastcheap, London, which is the new center for Amos Trust under its director, Rev. Chris Rose. Garth is also an honorary canon of St George's Episcopal Cathedral, Jerusalem.

In 2006 Garth was given special creditation by the House of Poets in Ramallah, West Bank, for his "positive attitude towards the Palestinian people and their struggle towards freedom and justice." He is also a patron of the Palestine Solidarity Campaign. For eight years Garth was on the board of Umthombo Street Children project in Durban, South Africa.

Garth passionately believes that it is always time for people of all faiths, or none, to speak up and call for justice, reaffirming the dignity, rights and value of each human being made in the image of God.

For news about The Garth Hewitt Foundation and Garth's ongoing work see www.garthhewitt.org.

www.gingerdog-records.com